Day by Day
through the Gospel of

MARK

Day by Day
through the Gospel of
MARK
A Devotional Bible Study

Merrill and Olga Gilbertson

Augsburg
MINNEAPOLIS

Day by Day through the Gospel of Mark
A Devotional Bible Study

Interior design: Judy Gilats, Peregrine Publications
Cover design: Eric Walljasper
Cover photo: SPG International/Larry West

Library of Congress Cataloging-in-Publication Data

Gilbertson, Merrill T.
    Day by day through the gospel of Mark : a devotional Bible study /
Merrill and Olga Gilbertson.
      p.   cm.
    Includes bibliographical references.
    ISBN 0-8066-2614-3 (alk. paper) :
      1. Bible. N.T. Mark—Meditations.   2. Bible. N.T. Mark—Study.
    3. Devotional calendars.   I. Gilbertson, Olga, 1913-
    II. Title.
    BS2585.4.G55   1993
    226.3'06—dc20   92-32116
                                                                  CIP

Manufactured in the U.S.A.   AF 9-2614

97   96   95   94   93   1   2   3   4   5   6   7   8   9   10

A Tribute to Grandpa

When I was seven my grandpa was my best friend. If problems arose, he was there to push them away and leave room for the sun to shine. Grandpa would tell me stories of a mystical place where even tomboys like me were beautiful. We went for long, slow walks while he filled my heart with laughter over his "classic" grandpa jokes. There was a spring in his walk like a child's first Christmas, and he seemed to have the world to live for. That was before the disease.

Suddenly the sun stopped shining and the rain started pouring. His cheerful blue eyes became cloudy and confused. Long walks gave way to endless questions. Instead of stories of faraway lands, he asked me who I was and looked confused when I replied, "I'm your granddaughter." Grandpa had become a prisoner trapped by a disease so unknown. Like a captive inside himself, he fought to be free of the chains on his soul. When he was released from the bondage of this world, I said good-bye to the best grandpa a girl could have.

Sonja Anderson

WITH GRATITUDE

I thank my dear heavenly Father for his grace and mercy in Christ Jesus and for the enlightenment of the Holy Spirit. I cannot of my own reason or strength believe in Jesus Christ or come to him.

I thank the Lord for my Christ-centered home in which the love of Jesus was lived. What a blessing to have a consecrated father and mother who nurtured ten children! What love, what fun, what joy, and what visions and security in the Word.

I still marvel at how the Lord molded Merrill's life and my life. He brought us together and helped us see the impossible become the possible—school, books, trips to the Holy Land, family, college students, and praying parishioners.

I offer deep gratitude to our three daughters, Mary, Ruth, and Lois, and their husbands, who have loved, encouraged, and prayed me through this study.

Thank you also to Samih, Awad, and Zahi Ismir who brought the land of Jesus closer to Merrill and me.

I thank God for the growth and joy in the Word with the Waldorf College students and faculty from 1949 to 1958, especially president Dr. Morton Nielsen, who had the vision to allow Merrill to teach the Bible instead of books about the Bible.

My deep appreciation goes to Norman and Evan Hagfors who urged me to get this Bible study published, helped me with the initial steps, and encouraged me professionally and financially all along the way. Evan patiently and hourly typed and retyped the first draft from my scribbled pages without a grumble. Rick and Noreen Rickenbach were staunch encouragers in writing and teaching. "Oh, you can do it. Merrill would want you to!" Thank you also to the fun Bible Study Prayer Group at Dr. Arthur and Marg Hall's home for their love and encouragement.

Blessing on my many prayer warriors—too many to list them all. However, two especially—Randi Oksnevad and Nina Sakariason—encouraged, loved, and held me up in prayer every day for four years. They were happy when I completed a lesson and laughed with me when I bogged down.

Only the Lord can bless the many who evaluated my lessons, but a special thanks goes to the staff and students at the Laymen's Ministry Training Center where we have experienced the gospel.

May I say love and thanks to my heartwarming encourager and editor, Irene Getz. How refreshing to work with such competent, dedicated Christians as Robert Moluf, editorial director of Augsburg Books, and Irene Getz.

PREFACE

What a joy Merrill and I had studying the Word. Even before our marriage, Merrill insisted that more education would be our aim. Inwardly I laughed, but in 1949 we journeyed three thousand miles with two little children—Mary four, and Ruth two—to the Biblical Seminary in New York. We slept in a tent on the way and cooked our meals in God's beautiful outdoors. Fortunately, when we got to New York, we were able to live in a parsonage. What a challenge to study with pastors of all denominations and teachers who challenged and inspired us. But Merrill was my greatest teacher. "Let's put away all our preconceived ideas, Olga, and see Jesus," he said. "We aren't the Word; we are vehicles!"

Merrill promised his students at Waldorf College and his Bible students at Grace Lutheran in Albert Lea and at First Lutheran in Minneapolis that a concise study of the Gospel of Mark would follow the three books he had already written. However, Alzheimer's disease caught up with him and he was unable to keep his promise. After his death in 1988, I had the feeling that God was calling me to complete Merrill's work. Although I resisted at first, I finally obeyed and said, "Lord, I'm not a writer, but I'll try." Through study, Merrill's notes, prayer, and many tears I began. Finally the lessons began to take form. Would they be simple, clear enough as Merrill would want them, an inspiration and help for that person who lived thirty miles from any class or teacher? Were they true to the Word, too argumentative, too intellectual, or too ambiguous? Would an individual see Jesus, accept him, live for him?

Hence, I'm approaching this study from a traditional stance. I'm assuming that John Mark was the author and I'm not worried about newer, historical-critical speculations concerning the author, sources of sayings, editing by later hands, or other intellectual inquiries. Merrill used to say, "It's not just knowing the Word—we must live it." So his desire would be that this study "go out only to the glory of Jesus."

Have fun and blessings.

Merrill and Olga

PREPARATION
1:1-13

PROCLAMATION
1:14-8:30

THE BEGINNING

UNIT 1 – 1:1-13

- 1:1 Greatest Title
- 1:2-8 Greatest Forerunner
- 1:9-11 Greatest Confirmation
- 1:12-13 Greatest Confrontation

GROWING POPULARITY

UNIT 2 – 1:14-45

- 1:14-15 Repent, Believe
- 1:16-20 Follow Me
- 1:21-28 With Authority
- 1:29-31 Simon's Mother-In-Law
- 1:32-34 Sunset Scene
- 1:35-39 Sunrise Scene
- 1:40-45 Loving the Unloveable

GROWING OPPOSITION

UNIT 3 – 2:1-3:6

- 2:1-12 First Opposition
- 2:13-14 Call of Levi
- 2:15-17 Second Opposition
- 2:18-20 Third Opposition
- 2:21-22 New, Not Old
- 2:23-28 Fourth Opposition
- 3:1-6 Fifth Opposition

PROCLAMATION

GROWING ORGANIZATION

UNIT 4 – 3:7-35

- 3:7-12 Withdrawal
- 3:13-19a The Twelve
- 3:19b-27 Head-on-Collision
- 3:28-30 The Unpardonable Sin
- 3:31-35 Family of God

PARABLES

UNIT 5 – 4:1-34

- 4:1-9 Receptivity of the Word
- 4:10-12 Secret of the Kingdom
- 4:13-20 Explanation
- 4:21-25 Use of the Word
- 4:26-29 Growth of the Word
- 4:30-32 Power of the Word
- 4:33-34 Many Parables

MIRACLES

UNIT 6 – 4:35-5:43

- 4:35-41 Power Over Nature
- 5:1-13 Power Over Demons
- 5:14-20 The Departure
- 5:21-24a Jairus
- 5:24b-34 Power Over Sickness
- 5:35-43 Power Over Death

PROCLAMATION

INTERNSHIP

UNIT 7 – 6:1-56

- 6:1-6a Nazareth
- 6:6b-13 Two by Two
- 6:14-16 Who is Jesus?
- 6:17-29 Herod
- 6:30-44 Feeding the 5000
- 6:45-46 Time for Quiet
- 6:47-52 Walking on the Sea
- 6:53-56 Gennesaret

INTENSIVE TRAINING

UNIT 8 – 7:1-8:30

- 7:1-8 Unwashed Hands
- 7:9-13 Corban
- 7:14-16 Listen
- 7:17-23 Within & Without
- 7:24-30 Gentile Woman
- 7:31-37 Be Opened
- 8:1-10 Feeding the 4000
- 8:11-13 Request for a Sign
- 8:14-21 Yeast of Pharisees
- 8:22-26 Restored Sight
- 8:27-30 The Great Confession

PASSION 8:31-16:20

CRISIS WEEK   *JOURNEY TO JERUSALEM*

UNIT 9 – 8:31-9:29
8:31-33 Jesus Christ
8:34-9:1 The Disciples' Cross
9:2-8 The Great Confirmation
9:9-13 The Great Prophet
9:14-29 The Great Failure

UNIT 10 – 9:30-10:52
9:30-32 The Second Announcement
9:33-37 What's the Greatest?
9:38-41 For or Against?
9:42-48 Millstone
9:49-50 Salt
10:1 Judea
10:2-9 Divorce
10:10-12 Marriage
10:13-16 Children
10:17-22 Rich Young Man
10:23-27 Kingdom of God
10:28-31 Hundredfold
10:32-34 The Third Announcement
10:35-40 James and John
10:41-45 Not to be Served, but to Serve
10:46-52 Blind Bartimaeus

PASSION

CLASHES IN THE TEMPLE   *FUTURE EVENTS*

UNIT 11 – 11:1-12:44
11:1-10 Triumphant Entry
11:11 Temple Inspection
11:12-14 Jesus Curses a Fig Tree
11:15-19 Cleansing of the Temple
11:20-24 Fig Tree Withered
11:25-26 Forgive
11:27-33 First Clash
12:1-11 Vineyard
12:12 Fear of the Crowd
12:13-17 Second Clash
12:18-23 Third Clash
12:24-27 God of the Living
12:28-34 Fourth Clash
12:35-37 Son of David
12:38-40 Long Robes and Prayers
12:41-44 The Widow's Coin

UNIT 12 – 13:1-37
13:1-2 Not One Stone
13:3-8 Signs in the World
13:9-13 Signs in Local Community
13:14-23 Signs in the Church
13:24-27 Signs in the Sky
13:28-31 Signs in the Fig Tree
13:32-37 Keep Alert

PASSION

ARREST AND TRIAL   *CRUCIFIXION AND RESURRECTION*

UNIT 13 – 14:1-15:15
14:1-2 Plot to Kill
14:3-9 The Anointing
14:10-11 Judas's Plot
14:12-16 The Passover
14:17-21 Is It I?
14:22-25 The Lord's Supper
14:26-31 Prediction
14:32-42 Gethsemane
14:43-50 Betrayal
14:51-52 Young Man
14:53-65 Trial Before High Priest
14:66-72 The Denial
15:1-5 Trial Before Pilate
15:6-15 Barabbas

UNIT 14 – 15:16-16:20
15:16-20 The Mockery
15:21-24 Golgotha
15:25-32 The Crucifixion
15:33-39 Death
15:40-41 The Women
15:42-47 Burial
16:1-8 The Resurrection
16:9-11 First Appearance
16:12-13 Second Appearance
16:14-18 Go, Tell
16:19-20 Ascension

INTRODUCTION

"Go into all the world and proclaim the good news to the whole creation." Mark 16:15

We have no need to gather up all the Bible commentaries in the world, useful though they be in order to study God's Word. If we will just sit down and spend time with the Lord and his Word, the Holy Spirit will make the words come alive, providing insights that will surprise and challenge us. No experience is required! "Open my eyes, so that I may behold wondrous things out of your law" (Ps. 119:18).

The Gospel of Mark is quick, to the point, and unsurpassed in action. Through this book, Mark gives the world a picture of Christ, the Servant. He portrays Christ as the Mighty Deliverer who came "not to be served, but to serve."

Christ's service is in deep harmony with the heroism and self-sacrifice needed in that day as well as today. We may marvel at the swift changing scenes that capture our attention in this book. Yet Mahatma Gandhi said, "You Christians make me tired. You have a book that is dynamite, but you use it as if it were great literature." May our study of this fascinating book refresh our awareness of Christ our Savior and arouse us to deeper devotion to this Servant.

In your study, please refrain from simply writing answers to the questions. Rather, meditate, study, and allow the Holy Spirit to quicken your understanding of the passage. Remember, the Holy Spirit may interpret something differently to you than to me; none of us has the only insight. Therefore, please do not read the leader's guide before you have really studied the paragraph in Mark for the day. One paragraph may seem like a small amount, but consider what a woman who was dying of cancer told me. She said, "It was when I began to learn that my physical strength could grasp only a small portion at a time—one paragraph, one verse—that God gave me deep insight, direction, strength, and joy for the day."

This paragraph-by-paragraph study of Mark is designed to help the ordinary person develop a regular habit of personal Bible study. It will help you understand Mark's point of view. It will help you ask questions that broaden your understanding: What is here? Why is it placed here?

Is it giving a contrast or offering interpretation? Such questions will heighten your ability to observe: stop, look, listen!

Make this study your own. Move at your own pace. Take two days, if necessary, to complete one lesson. The regularity of your study counts more than the speed of your study. As you study, listen for the prompting of the Spirit. Write notes in your Bible as well as in a notebook. This will help you establish ideas in your mind, and give you something to return to as you develop your thoughts about the Scripture being studied. The Holy Spirit works through a pen or pencil.

The method of study is the same every day:

1. Record the date studied in your notebook. It's good discipline to note your progress.

2. Pray! Get into a receptive frame of mind. To get started, you might like to use the prayer for the week as you begin each lesson.

3. Start memorizing the verse for the unit. Copy the verse on a three-by-five card. Put it on your refrigerator, mirror, or other place that is highly visible to you. When you repeat a verse for several days, stressing the verbs, it will become more meaningful to you. Dr. Jacob Tanner, a Bible teacher at Waldorf College, used to say, "Let the verbs speak." These portions of Scripture you memorize will become a treasure-house for Christian living.

4. Study the day's lesson. Observation comes first as this is the most important part of your study and growth. Search the Scriptures, one paragraph a day. Read the paragraph several times and record your observations in your notebook before answering the questions. Take note of the continuity of the passage and the striking words and phrases, ideas, thoughts, impressions, and insights that the Holy Spirit gives you. Let's take a short paragraph as an example, Mark 4:26-29, from Lesson 29. Here are five observations:

a. Jesus compared the kingdom of God to scattering the seed, the Word.

b. As I sleep and rise, I know Jesus takes care of the growing.

c. I don't know *how* such growing happens, but God does.

d. The Word in a person's heart often grows slowly (stalk, head, full grain).

e. When the grain is ripe, Jesus takes care of the harvest.

Now turn to the questions. They are not profound but simply are a guide to see the "who, what, when, where, and why." Use a dictionary as needed. Look up all Bible references given in the lesson. If the lesson seems too much for one day, just do what you can and go back to it the next day.

I refer especially to two books: *The Way It Was in Bible Times* by Merrill Gilbertson (now out of print, but available in some libraries) and *Prayer* by Ole Hallesby (Augsburg). You may find it helpful to have those books at hand. If Merrill's book is unavailable, a good Bible dictionary is an option. A prayer thought at the end of each lesson may set the tone for talking to the Father. Discussion questions at the end of each lesson are intended especially for study groups, but useful for personal reflection as well. In a group, each person could study several paragraphs and come ready for the discussion questions.

5. Focus on the main thought. Listen! What is the Holy Spirit saying to you from this passage? As often as possible, insert your own name into the words of Scripture. For example, "God so loved 'Olga' that he gave. . . ."

6. Think about the challenge raised in the day's lesson and write it into a prayer. Pray the prayer for yourself, for each member of your family, or for your friends. Often we become so involved in our study that we forget to assimilate the power of God's Word by taking time to pray. The lessons are short, so you will not be tempted to neglect prayer. Learn to pray the scriptures!

7. Make the notebook your personal study and prayer diary. List your concerns and joys. Be specific! Can you discipline yourself to pray out loud? It takes willpower! Our twentieth-century life spells "stress." Yet, in this Gospel, Jesus is the calm center of every situation. Give him your time. Allow him to call you to peaceful action throughout the day as a result of being *with him!*

8. Let the Gospel of Mark enrich, enlighten, and change you! Use it as a guide in your daily life and share the blessings with others.

9. The New Revised Standard Version (NRSV) is used throughout the study.

LESSON 1

Father, I know your Word is powerful! I sometimes have such glorious dreams of what I can do for your kingdom, but my days often lack vision and seem so mundane, so commonplace. Now I am realizing that the key isn't what I do, but what your Word does through me. So your Word must have priority if my dreams are to come true.

Oh, how I pray that you will keep me faithful in this study of the Gospel of Mark. Help me to stand on tiptoe in expectation, as I assimilate your Word and look for my dreams to open up. In Jesus' name. Amen.

Bible verse: "For the Son of Man came not to be served but to serve and to give his life as a ransom for many." Mark 10:45

Read the verse several times, preferably out loud, and write it on a card. Place the card where you will see it frequently so you can work on memorizing the verse.

To study a book, we need to know something about the author. Read Acts 12:1-17. Focus your thoughts on verse 12.

Who was Mark?
Why might we think his father was dead?
What was Mark's other name?
What was happening in his home?
What facts indicate that Mark's home was large, and that his was a family of means?
What was Mary able to afford (see verse 13)?
Write down four adjectives you would use to describe Mary.
How might such prayer meetings have influenced Mark?
What is this lesson telling you?
Do your home and church meet the requirements of a house of prayer? If not, why not?

Today's challenge:
As we hear from Christian leaders, lay people, and even pastors, we are amazed to learn how little time we spend alone on our knees in

prayer, not only for our families, nation, and church, but also for the brokenness, emptiness, and hurts of those around us.

Write today's challenge into a prayer. For example: Father, you know the needs in our home. Give me and my husband, wife, brother, sister, roommate, or friend a deep desire for a definite prayer life. Help me to be faithful in prayer; make me teachable! What attitude of defeat, insecurity, criticism, or busyness do I need to face?

Thank you for the insights Mark will give me each day, Father. Help me to be faithful. I know you faithfully wait for me to take time to be with you.

Other prayers: Your own
Examples: Gift of listening . . .
Thanks for a blessing . . .
Courage for my son . . .
A job for . . .
Integrity for our nation

Questions for discussion or reflection:
How have you developed a daily devotional period so you can be the extension of God's hands?
What three forces make daily devotions so difficult for you?
Why is listening to God so important?

LESSON 2

Be still! Pray the prayer from Lesson 1 and review the Bible verse.
We can learn more about Mark's background by studying what the Bible says about his companions. Some scholars even say Mark wrote his Gospel through Peter's eyes!

What does Peter call Mark in 1 Pet. 5:13?
Who was Mark's cousin? (Col. 4:10)
With whom did John Mark travel? (Acts 12:25; 13:2-5)
Could John Mark take the pressure of their active ministry?

What did he do? (Acts 13:13)

How did Barnabas feel about Mark later? (Acts 15:36-40)

Were Paul and Mark ever reconciled? (2 Tim. 4:11)

What other Gospel writer did Mark have the privilege of knowing? (2 Tim. 4:11 and Philemon 1:23-24)

Use your imagination. What do you think Luke and Mark may have talked about? (Philemon 1:23)

Write down the names of Mark's coworkers. (Philemon 1:23-24)

Try to figure out how many of the twenty-seven New Testament books Mark's friends wrote.

Today's challenge:

What friends enrich your spiritual life?

In what ways do you befriend others?

Write today's challenge as a prayer: Father, I thank you for . . .

Other prayers:

Questions for discussion or reflection:

To what friends are you an encouraging Barnabas?

When have you been a Peter to another believer?

Many believe that Peter told the gospel to Mark. Who nudged you toward your belief in the gospel message?

LESSON 3

Quiet your heart by again reviewing the prayer and Bible verse in Lesson 1. What message did Mark want to communicate in his Gospel? (It is found in Mark 10:45, the *key verse* of the Gospel.)

Mark wanted to bring the saving message of Christ to the world. Jesus' coming had not only changed Mark's life, but also the lives of his family and companions. While the other Gospel writers were concerned about reaching the Jews (Matthew), the Greeks (Luke), and those who might believe (John), Mark wrote to those who knew Jesus or had heard of him (I like to think he wrote for the Romans too). Mark used a brief, often blunt, and forceful style. He moved into action and presented Jesus' ministry chronologically, which was an excellent way to reach his intended audience.

The Romans were the masters of the world in Mark's time. They gloried in the bloody exhibitions of their gladiators. Often a thousand gladiators would fight to their deaths in a one-hundred-day period. The Romans may have said, "We know nothing about and could care less about your Jewish traditions, but we would love to know the plain truth about Jesus, who did so many wonders and served everyone. Who was he? Why did he go to his death so willingly?" Notice how Mark challenged the Gentile minds of his day, and ours, in the key verse:

> "For the Son of Man came not to be served but to serve, and to give his life as a ransom for many (Mark 10:45)."

Repeat this verse three times out loud, stressing the different parts of speech each time. Stress the verbs the first time, the nouns the second time, and *for*, *but*, and *and* the third time.

What do the conjunctions *for* and *but* add to the meaning of the verse?
What does the "Son of Man" mean?
Where is the "Son of Man" used in the Old Testament?
What three action words describe the Son of Man's life? Underline them.

Today's challenge:
What difference do the verbs *come*, *serve*, and *give* make in your life?
What mental picture does the word *ransom* create in your mind?

Write today's challenge as a prayer:

Other prayers:

Questions for discussion or reflection:
There isn't anything passive about the three verbs Mark uses to describe Jesus' life, is there?
In what area of your life are you passive or active? Home? Church? Community? Government?

LESSON 4

The Father is waiting! Take time to be with him as you meditate on the prayer and Bible verse in Lesson 1.

The Holy Spirit used Mark's mind to write a tremendous, precise Gospel. The Gospel of Mark can be arranged into three divisions according to the key verse.

Preparation	Proclamation	Passion
(to come)	(to serve)	(to give)
1:1-13	1:14—8:30	8:31—16:20

The three divisions are divided into 14 units and 124 paragraphs that retell the active, orderly events in Jesus' life. This system may seem confusing at first, but be patient. You will catch on in time.

Our first division is Preparation and the first unit is The Beginning. Due to Mark's brevity, the first unit covers the same verses as the first division (Mark 1:1-13). Today we study the first short paragraph, Mark 1:1: "The beginning of the good news of Jesus Christ, the Son of God." Since this paragraph has no verb, we will call it "Greatest Title."

Division 1: Preparation, Mark 1:1-13
Unit 1: The Beginning, Mark 1:1-13
Paragraph 1: Greatest Title, Mark 1:1

What does a beginning mean to you?
Where else in the Bible do you remember a beginning?
Of what beginning in relation to Jesus Christ did Mark write?
How does Mark's beginning differ from the beginnings written about in John 1:2; 17:5, and Col. 1:17?
What is the good news?
What does "Jesus" mean? (Matt. 1:21)
What does "Messiah" mean? (John 1:41)
What does the "Son of God" mean? (John 1:34)
Remember, the good news is Jesus Christ! How often do you hear his powerful name?

Today's challenge:
Mark said he was writing about the beginning of the good news. How are you continuing the gospel, the good news, of Jesus Christ among your family? Friends? And in church? Be specific.

Write today's challenge as a prayer:

Other prayers:

Questions for discussion or reflection:
If it depended on your witness, how far would the gospel reach? How can we help each other continue the gospel?

LESSON 5

Pause to review the prayer and Bible verse in Lesson 1.

Division 1: Preparation, Mark 1:1-13
Unit 1: Beginning, Mark 1:1-13
Paragraph 2: Greatest Forerunner, Mark 1:2-8

Read Mark 1:2-8 and record five observations. Here are five possible observations: Quote from the Old Testament, all the people, John is an interesting character, John is humble, difference in baptism.

Mark believed that Jesus Christ was King. As King, Jesus had a forerunner—one who prepared the way for Jesus. Hence, Mark included John the Baptist in the Preparation division. He drew from portions of Isaiah and Malachi to tell about this forerunner in Mark 1:2-3. (Remember, Isaiah wrote approximately 750 years before Christ!)

In Mark 1:2-3, who is the "I"? The "messenger"? Who is the "you" whom the messenger will precede? What will the messenger do? Whose "voice" will cry out?
What was John's message?
What did John's dress and eating habits say about him?

Do you think the crowds gathered because John was different?
How would you welcome John the Baptist into your home?
Why did John say what he did about the Son of God's sandals?
Was John a successful forerunner?
Why do you think Mark began his Gospel with John the Baptist and not Jesus?
What did John's baptism with water accomplish?

Today's challenge:
Read Mark 1:7-8, substituting the name *Jesus* for the words *one, he,* and *his* in the quotation. How will Jesus "baptize" you and me? What does that mean to you?
Review the paragraph. How does God keep his promise? What comfort does that give you?

Write today's challenge as a prayer:

Other prayers:

Questions for discussion or reflection:
What spiritual wilderness have you been in? How did that wilderness experience help you grow?
What does the word *repentance* mean to you? Is that word in common use today?
What unique, divine personality do you have the privilege of directing people toward?

LESSON 6

Relax. Breathe in and out slowly three times. Meditate on the prayer and Bible verse in Lesson 1.

Division 1: Preparation, Mark 1:1-13
Unit 1: The Beginning, Mark 1:1-13
Paragraph 3: Greatest Confirmation, Mark 1:9-11

Study verses 9-11 and record five observations. Focus on the events and their importance. What a beautiful passage this is! Here we see the inauguration, the ordination, of Jesus into his ministry. Read Luke 1:5-25, 57-80 to find out more about John, the one who announced Jesus' coming and the one who baptized him. "In those days" means that John the Baptist was at the height of his ministry.

At that time, in what city did Jesus live?
Where did Jesus go to be baptized by John?
How far did Jesus walk (from Nazareth to the Jordan River)? (See map on page 240.)
What kind of a town was Nazareth? (Look in a Bible dictionary.)
Jesus moved as the Father gave him guidance. He was always in the Father's will.
What astounding role did God give Jesus?
What did John see when he baptized Jesus? (John 1:32-34)

Some people watching Jesus' baptism may have remembered the prophet's words in Isa. 64:1. What a sight they witnessed! Mark made it clear that something glorious, something new, took place that day! In this paragraph we see evidence of the powerful Trinity.
Identify Jesus, the Father, and the Holy Spirit in this event?
What confirmation did God give his Son?
Why was Jesus baptized?

Today's challenge:
You were baptized into the powerful Trinity.
What strength do you accept from that name?
Have you thanked the Lord for the gift of baptism?
What does baptism mean in your life?

Write today's challenge as a prayer:

Other prayers:

Questions for discussion and reflection:
Examine and analyze the depth of your baptism as described in Gal. 3:27, Rom. 6:4, and Col. 2:12.
How is Jesus' baptism the opening of his divine, messianic passion?

LESSON 7

Nestle in God's love. Once more, pray the prayer and review the Bible verse in Lesson 1.

Division 1: Preparation, Mark 1:1-13
Unit 1: The Beginning, Mark 1:1-13
Paragraph 4: Greatest Confrontation, Mark 1:12-13

Slowly read verses 12-13 and record five observations about Jesus' wilderness experience. Reread the paragraph and underline the striking and noteworthy words.

Before Jesus could begin his ministry he had to face Satan (Matt. 4:1-11, Luke 4:1-13).
From whom had Jesus received assurance and power before he met Satan?
Why do you think Mark said so little about Jesus' temptation?
Who descended on Jesus in the previous paragraph?
Who drove Jesus into the wilderness? When? Why do you think this occurred?
How long was Jesus in the wilderness? (Compare Gen. 7:17, Exod. 16:35, Num. 14:33, and Acts 1:3.)
In your notebook, list four noteworthy observations about Jesus' time in the wilderness.
How do you identify with the things that happened to him?
Who is Satan?
What is your most vulnerable area for Satan's attacks? (1 Pet. 5:8)
Do you have angels ministering to you? (Heb. 1:14, Ps. 34:7)
What difference does it make in your life that Jesus met and conquered Satan?
How long does forty days seem to you?

Can you outline the study, Mark 1:1-13, thus far? Organize the paragraph names in your mind, and notice how Mark included just enough about Jesus' "beginning" to intrigue the Romans (and us).

Today's challenge:
To appreciate the masterful beauty of Mark's first four paragraphs, think about the four or five most important events in your life. Then think how you would describe those events in a few paragraphs.

Write today's challenge as a prayer:

Other prayers:

Questions for discussion or reflection:
Why is Jesus' temptation recorded in Mark's Gospel?
What enables you to face temptation? What is your greatest weapon against temptation?
Why are trials necessary?
Why are temptations detrimental to us only when we succumb to sin?

LESSON 8

Father, I am surprised at your Son's popularity! Was he popular because he was a realist absolutely helpless without you? When I struggle and try to do things in my own strength, I need to remember the words Jesus said, "I can do nothing on my own" (John 5:30). Father, I know it's one thing to know and another to relinquish. Help me to be absolutely helpless, to give you my busy adequacy, and to live in the joy of your grace. Help me to see in these lessons why Jesus was so needed and how he was an extension of your mighty hand at all times. Mentally, I know he is stretching out his hand to touch me too, but I need to know spiritually. Amen.

Bible verse: "Moved with pity, Jesus stretched out his hand and touched him, and said to him, 'I do choose. Be made clean.'" Mark 1:41

Division 2: Proclamation, Mark 1:14—8:30
Unit 2: Growing Popularity, Mark 1:14-45
Paragraph 1: Repent, Believe, Mark 1:14-15

Read verses 14-15 and record five observations. Notice we begin the Proclamation division.

With Jesus' appearance, God's kingdom is at hand. As soon as Jesus steps on the scene, things begin to happen.

Proclaim means to make known. Jesus proclaims his message by voice, expression, word, and action. In doing so, his popularity grows by leaps and bounds.

When does Mark say Jesus began his public ministry? Where did his public ministry begin?
Why was John imprisoned? (Mark 6:17-29)
What is the "good news"?
Write down the four points of Jesus' first proclamation.
What does "the time is fulfilled" mean? (Gal. 4:4-5)
Name three or four world conditions that made the coming of God's kingdom possible.
What is the kingdom of God?
Where is it?
Who had preached this message of repentance before? (Mark 1:4)
What were the Jews longing for?
Whom should they have recognized?

Today's challenge:
Are we afraid of the word *repent* in our churches today? Where are you as to daily repentance and believing?

Write today's challenge as a prayer:

Other prayers:

Questions for discussion or reflection:
How do believers today continue to proclaim John's and Jesus' message of repentance?
When did you last discuss repentance with someone or hear a sermon on repentance?

LESSON 9

Relax. Pray the prayer and review the Bible verse from Lesson 8.

Division 2: Proclamation, Mark 1:14—8:30
Unit 2: Growing Popularity, Mark 1:14-45
Paragraph 2: Follow Me, Mark 1:16-20

Study verses 16-20 and record five observations. What sea was so important in Jesus' life?

Notice how popular Jesus had become in verses 18 and 20. Underline the words *left* and *followed* in your Bible. What does this invitation demand?

Begin to tie these paragraphs together. If the good news (verses 1, 14-15) was so tremendously important, Jesus needed bearers of that message.

Whom did he choose?
Why are the four so interesting?
Was this the first time these brothers had seen Jesus? (John 1:35-42)
Materially, how were these brothers different?
What was Jesus' call and promise?
How faithfully did these four follow Jesus?

Do you think those who followed Jesus talked about Jesus' call among themselves or with their parents? Imagine what their conversation may have been like! If you are in a group, talk about this possible conversation; if you are studying alone, think about it imaginatively. Have fun!

Today's challenge:
How are you going to follow Jesus in your life—not tomorrow, but today?
How are you helping others to follow him?

Write today's challenge as a prayer:

Other prayers:

Questions for discussion or reflection:
How do you relate to a person in another church or in a cult? How do you relate to an atheist?
Are they worthy to follow Jesus?
Are you and I worthy?
Are some of us more worthy of following Jesus than others?

LESSON 10

Be still. Relax in Jesus' love. Pray the prayer and review the Bible verse from Lesson 8.

Division 2: Proclamation, Mark 1:14—8:30
Unit 2: Growing Popularity, Mark 1:14-45
Paragraph 3: With Authority, Mark 1:21-28

Read verses 21-28 and record five observations. As you study, remember that when Jesus appeared on the scene, things began to happen. In this paragraph we see a power struggle between Jesus and Satan.
What city are they in?
What day is it?
Where in the city are they?
It's important to know more about Capernaum and the role of the synagogue in Jewish life. Use a good Bible dictionary or encyclopedia to answer the following questions.
What is the city of Capernaum known for?
What is a synagogue?
Why is a scribe referred to? What was the Sabbath?
Why could Jesus teach in this synagogue?

Jesus not only had a message, but also he taught with authority.
What does it mean to teach with authority?

What is an unclean spirit?

List in your notebook six characteristics of demons that are revealed in this paragraph.

In what ways does Jesus identify with the longing of the human soul?

What amazes you about the demon's statement to Jesus?

What pronoun does the demon use in verse 24?

Why didn't Jesus want the evil spirit to reveal Jesus' identity?

Why did the spirit leave unwillingly?

How did the healing affect the crowd?

Underline the words that indicate Jesus' growing popularity (verses 22, 27-28). Use your imagination to see every eye fixed on Jesus in rapt attention. In Jesus' time, everyone was afraid of demons—even the Romans. You can imagine what an unforgettable scene this was. Notice how the words *at once* contribute to the rapid progress of Mark's Gospel. We really see Christ in action.

What should the crowd have asked instead of "What is this?"

Today's challenge:

Do you use the authority of Jesus' words in your life? Do you use them in your prayers for others?

Write today's challenge as a prayer:

Other prayers:

Questions for discussion or reflection:

What do we think about demons today?

How do we handle them?

What does Jesus need to cast out of your life?

LESSON 11

Be still and pray the prayer in Lesson 8. Review the Bible verse. Are the verbs becoming more vivid and meaningful to you?

Division 2: Proclamation, Mark 1:14—8:30
Unit 2: Growing Popularity, Mark 1:14-45
Paragraph 4: Simon's Mother-in-Law, Mark 1:29-31

Read verses 29-31 and record five observations. Underline the words *then*, *at once*, and *as soon as*.
Do you see how quickly Mark moved through this Gospel of action? Jesus truly applies his gospel to daily life.
Why do you think Jesus left the synagogue?
In what city is the synagogue?
Who is Simon? (John 1:42)
Do you think Simon and Andrew had a purpose in asking Jesus to come to their home? What was it?

Notice the woman's fever in Luke 4:38-39. What word describes the disciples' act? Shut your eyes, and try to picture the scene—the fevered mother, the anxious family, the eager disciples, and calm, compassionate Christ!
In what ways does this healing differ from that of verses 21-29?
What actions show Jesus' compassion?
How did Mark emphasize the completeness of the woman's healing?

Today's challenge:
From what do you need to be healed today? A heavy heart? Bitterness? Jealousy? Procrastination? Busyness? Worry? Physical illness? Materialism? An unbalanced life-style?
How are you an extension of Christ's healing power?

Write today's challenge as a prayer:

Other prayers:

Questions for discussion or reflection:
Do you dare to pray for healing?
Why doesn't everyone who prays for healing receive it?
Have you prayed the memory verse for yourself and others?

LESSON 12

Be still, and pour out your dependence on Jesus. Pray the prayer and review the Bible verse in Lesson 8.

Division 2: Proclamation, Mark 1:14—8:30
Unit 2: Growing Popularity, Mark 1:14-45
Paragraph 5: Sunset Scene, Mark 1:32-34

Study verses 32-34 and record five observations about Jesus' popularity in the city. Visualize this scene. Jesus must have had a long day!
Why did Mark stress the time of day, evening, at sunset?
Why was there such a large crowd?
What kind of people were brought to Jesus?
What is Mark's graphic description of Jesus' popularity?
What words show us that demon possession is not a sickness?
What else did Mark reveal about the characteristics of demons?
What did Jesus tell the demons to do?
Are there demons today?

Recall the name of this unit. Underline the words that indicate Jesus' popularity: *brought ... all* (verse 32) and *whole city* (verse 33).

Today's challenge:
What stress surrounded Jesus. Notice how he handled it. How can your family be lifted to a higher level of daily living—even on the most stressful days?

Write today's challenge as a prayer:

Other prayers:

Questions for discussion or reflection:
What do you do when you're under great stress?
Does your reaction to people and circumstances make you miserable?
Are you responsible for your actions?

LESSON 13

Seek Jesus' presence as you review the prayer and Bible verse in Lesson 8.

Division 2: Proclamation, Mark 1:14—8:30
Unit 2: Growing Popularity, Mark 1:14-45
Paragraph 6: Sunrise Scene, Mark 1:35-39

Read verses 35-39 and record five observations about Jesus' commitment to doing the Father's will. Note the time and place.
What pressures could Jesus anticipate as a new day arrived?
Why did Jesus withdraw?
Compare Luke 9:18, 28.
What do you think Jesus prayed about?
Describe what the crowd was doing while Jesus prayed.
What was Peter's impatient statement? How I love Jesus' answer!
What was Jesus' mission?
What was Jesus' attitude toward popularity?
In what three ways did Jesus carry out evangelism?
How big do you think the province of Galilee was? (Refer to the map on page 240.)
Underline the words that indicate Jesus' popularity: *hunted* (verse 36), *everyone* (verse 37), and so forth.

Today's challenge:
Remember, it was Jesus' constant communion with his Father that gave his actions authority and power. Jesus surprises us by going to unexpected places and doing unexpected things. How are you doing as a friend to that "separated" father or mother, that lonesome child, that spouse of an alcoholic, that family whose breadwinner is unemployed, or that individual who suffers from racial or ethnic discrimination?

Write today's challenge as a prayer:

Other prayers:

Questions for discussion or reflection:
How do you prepare for each day?
How do you relate to those around you?
How do others relate to you?
Would arising "while it was still very dark" help you? Is your witness to others in proportion to the time you spend in prayer?

LESSON 14

Quiet yourself before God and pray the prayer and review the Bible verse in Lesson 8.

Division 2: Proclamation, Mark 1:14—8:30
Unit 2: Growing Popularity, Mark 1:14-45
Paragraph 7: Loving the Unlovable, Mark 1:40-45

Read verses 40-45 and record five observations about Jesus and the leper he healed.
Jesus performed hundreds upon hundreds of miracles. In this instance he brings healing to one of the most fearful situations of the day—leprosy! How the Romans must have shrunk from the leper. He was just as loathsome as the demoniac.

What is leprosy?
How did this social and religious outcast manage to come to Jesus?
Notice the verbs that describe the leper's actions. What do the leper's posture and statement reveal?
The leper seemed positive about Jesus' power to heal, but why did he doubt Jesus' willingness? (See Leviticus 13.)

Now record the compassionate steps in Jesus' healing. See how Jesus lavishes love on unlovely people!
What astonishing thing did Jesus do as he healed the leper?

What was the leper required to do before he could be restored to the Jewish community? (Leviticus 13-14)
What instructions did Jesus give to the leper after he healed him?
Why do you think the man disobeyed Jesus?
What resulted from his disobedience?

Today's challenge:
In Jesus' day, curing leprosy was as amazing as raising the dead, because the lepers were treated as if they were dead.
In what ways are we lepers?
How has Jesus touched us?
Does this lesson help you love God more?
How does it help you love others who are caught in the unforgiven leprosy of sin?

This is the end of Unit 2. Review the rapid action of Mark 1:14-45. Notice the evidence of divine love and its earthshaking power! In what ways do you see that the kingdom of God is at hand?

Write today's challenge as a prayer:

Other prayers:

Questions for discussion or reflection:
Popularity is the focus of this unit. What people today suffer from society's emphasis on popularity?
Do people today praise the faithful or the famous?
What occupies your mind—television and movie stars, work, leisure activities, or spiritual concerns?
What area of your life needs Jesus' touch?

LESSON 15

Father, thank you for the exciting Gospel of Mark. There is so much turmoil, so much hate, so much bitterness, so much hateful sin and debauchery in our world today that at times I want to give up and come home to you. But now I will be studying the opposition Jesus faced and will see how he achieved his goal. Was he able to touch people because he had one passion—to be a servant? Was he able to touch people because he faced opposition with a spirit of challenge and not a spirit of defeat or self-pity?

Lord, what do you want me to learn, to store in my heart today? I really want to learn. Do you want me to stand, take up my task, and walk? Amen.

Bible verse: "Stand up and take your mat and walk." Mark 2:9b

Division 2: Proclamation, Mark 1:14—8:30
Unit 3: Growing Opposition, Mark 2:1—3:6
Paragraph 1: First Opposition, Mark 2:1-12

We have finished Unit 2—Growing Popularity—in which Jesus' popularity had steadily increased. However, the religious rulers were becoming perturbed about four things: the crowds, the claims Jesus made about himself, Jesus' association with sinners, and his teaching in reference to their exacting laws. Hence the next unit of Mark's Gospel portrays the counterattack against Jesus and is called "Growing Opposition."

Read Mark 2:1-12 and record five observations. Focus on Jesus' actions and how various people responded to him. Get your directions straight.
Where had Jesus been?
Where was Jesus at the beginning of this paragraph?
Wasn't Nazareth Jesus' home? (Matt. 4:13)
What was Jesus' important work?
How did the paralytic's friends get him through the roof? (Luke 5:19)
What did Jesus see in these men?
What do you think the effort of the four men communicated to the paralytic?
Why didn't Jesus simply heal the man?
When the man faced Jesus, what spoke louder to Jesus than the man's physical condition?
In what ways is sin like paralysis?
Who opposed Jesus? How? Why?
What is blasphemy? What was the punishment for blasphemy? (Lev. 24:15-16)

What three instructions did Jesus give the man?
What test did Jesus give the crowd?
What tremendous name did Jesus call himself?
Why should the teachers of the law have known that Jesus was from God? (Isa. 35:5-7)

Today's challenge:
What obstacles must we break through to bring someone to Jesus? What is the most touching act someone has done for you? How can you apply the three instructions Jesus gave the man to the burdens in your daily life?

Write today's challenge as a prayer:

Other prayers:

Questions for discussion or reflection:
What significant insights into Jesus' kingdom did you discover in this lesson?
What would you have thought if you had been in that house in Capernaum?
If you were very ill, which four friends would help you?
When you see someone in trouble, do you act?
In what area of your life do you need to claim forgiveness—of God, of yourself?

LESSON 16

Be still. Pray the prayer and meditate on the love revealed in the Bible verse from Lesson 15.

Division 2: Proclamation, Mark 1:14—8:30
Unit 3: Growing Opposition, Mark 2:1—3:6
Paragraph 2: Call of Levi, Mark 2:13-14

Read 2:13-14 and record five observations.
Do you think this was the first time Levi had seen Jesus? (Matt. 9:9)

As you read this paragraph, try to imagine where Levi's office was and what it looked like. Refer to a Bible dictionary or encyclopedia to discover the tax collector's role in society.
Why were tax collectors disliked by the people?
With whom were tax collectors classed? (Matt. 9:11; 21:31)
Why do you think Jesus chose Levi?

The disciples had probably paid taxes to Levi:
How do you think they felt about Jesus' choice?
What did Levi's response cost him?
How is Levi's conversion like being raised from the dead?

Today's challenge:
Levi could have said, "I've got an awful reputation, Jesus. Won't I spoil your ministry?"
When have you ever felt that way?

Write today's challenge as a prayer:

Other prayers:

Questions for discussion or reflection:
Do you think Levi took advantage of people? How do people take advantage of others today?
What does it take to truly follow Jesus in our busy daily lives?

LESSON 17

Be still. Pray the prayer and review the Bible verse from Lesson 15. Do you remember the Bible verses from Units 1 and 2? If not, review them again. Let your family help you.

Division 2: Proclamation, Mark 1:14—8:30
Unit 3: Growing Opposition, Mark 2:1—3:6
Paragraph 3: Second Opposition, Mark 2:15-17

Read 2:15-17 and record five observations about Jesus' relationships with sinners. Notice the purpose of this event and the people who attended. Remember, this is the scene for the second opposition.

Who raised the opposition to Jesus?

To whom was the opposition expressed?

For what reason?

How many miles had this opposition traveled (if they came from Jerusalem) to raise their objections? (See map on page 240.)

What was Jesus' life philosophy regarding the righteous and the sinners?

How is Levi's (Matthew's) life a testimony to Christ's power?

Today's challenge:

How many so-called tax collectors and sinners do you consider as friends?

How has the Lord called you?

How can we be assured that we are disciples of Jesus? How was Levi assured of his discipleship?

Write today's challenge as a prayer:

Other prayers:

Questions for discussion or reflection:

Who has been a Levi in your life?

When were you a Levi?

What would your friends, neighbors, or family say to affirm your help to them?

LESSON 18

"Be still, and know that I am God!" (Ps. 46:10). Keep this verse in mind as you review the prayer and Bible verse from Lesson 15.

Division 2: Proclamation, Mark 1:14—8:30

Unit 3: Growing Opposition, Mark 2:1—3:6

Paragraph 4: Third Opposition, Mark 2:18-20

Paragraph 5: New, Not Old, Mark 2:21-22

Study verses 18-22 and record five observations.
Why wasn't John with his disciples? (Mark 1:14)

Refer to a good Bible dictionary or encyclopedia and learn all you can about fasting.
What is fasting and why is it brought up here?
Was Jesus opposed to fasting? (Matt. 6:16-18)

This is the setting for the third opposition.
Who raises the opposition?
To whom is the opposition directed?
For what reason?
How does the bridegroom story explain why the disciples didn't fast?
What does the "old cloak" represent?
What happens when new patches are put on old garments, or when new wine is put in old wineskins?
What is the new wine?
Is Jesus calling the Pharisees old wineskins?

Today's challenge:
How are we bound by old forms and traditions that may hinder others from seeing Christ?
Is each day a new beginning for you?
In what ways are you a new wineskin?
How do we become like old wineskins?

Write today's challenge as a prayer:

Other prayers:

Questions for discussion or reflection:
Why are so many people fasting today? What are their motives? Are all their motives good ones?
What are the benefits of fasting?
What do you think about fasting? Has fasting been a help in your life?
How are you boxed in by rules and laws instead of living in your new relationship with Christ?
Do you live with the realization that miracles and new ideas are all around you?

LESSON 19

Be still before God. Pray the prayer and review the Bible verse from Lesson 15.

Division 2: Proclamation, Mark 1:14—8:30
Unit 3: Growing Opposition, Mark 2:1—3:6
Paragraph 6: Fourth Opposition, Mark 2:23-28

Read verses 23-28 and record five observations. Focus on the differences between the Pharisees' view of the law and Jesus' view.

The Pharisees had fumed at Jesus' disregard for their burdensome rules regarding fasting. They tried to trap him about the Sabbath laws. What are the laws for the Sabbath? (Exod. 35:1-3)
Was it a sin for the disciples to pluck grain on the Sabbath? (Deut. 23:25, Lev. 19:9-10)

Study the *fourth opposition.*
Who raised the opposition?
To whom was the opposition directed?
For what reason?

Read 1 Sam. 21:1-6.
What is Jesus' clever defense against his attackers?
Why did Jesus refer to David?
Did Jesus admit that David and his companions broke God's law?
In what way does the Sabbath law differ from the laws of purity, honesty, or love? (Check a Bible dictionary.)
What does God say about the Sabbath? (Exod. 20:8-11, Deut. 5:12-15)

Today's challenge:
Can you think of three reasons why the Sabbath was made for people?
Are you happy with the way you spend the Sabbath in this age of stress?
Would you dare to invite Jesus to enjoy your Sabbath with you?
How might Jesus view your Sabbath activities?

Write today's challenge as a prayer:

Other prayers:

Questions for discussion or reflection:
How can you make the Sabbath more meaningful for your family?
In what ways do you judge the conduct of others on the Sabbath?
Is your Sabbath a day of rest and giving mercy or one of busyness?

LESSON 20

Be still. Are you living out the prayer and Bible verse from Lesson 15?

Division 2: Proclamation, Mark 1:14—8:30
Unit 3: Growing Opposition, Mark 2:1—3:6
Paragraph 7: Fifth Opposition, Mark 3:1-6

Read 3:1-6 and record five observations about this final opposition. In the foregoing paragraph, Jesus raised the ire of the scribes and Pharisees by declaring himself Lord of the Sabbath, which leads to the fifth opposition.
Who are the opposers?
How do they oppose Jesus? Why?
To understand Jesus' reasoning fully, read Matt. 12:9-12.
What did Jesus do before he healed the man?
Think about how patiently Jesus had explained their previous accusations. Why don't they answer him this time?
Did Jesus have a right to be angry with his accusers? Notice that Jesus did no visible work. He did not touch the man, but only told him to "stretch out your hand."
What was the Pharisees' greatest sin?
Try to imagine how happy the healed man was because he obeyed in faith and stretched out his hand!

Look up the Herodians in a good Bible dictionary or encyclopedia. Who were they? Why was it significant that the Pharisees went to them?

Think of the irony—the Jews accused Jesus of breaking the Sabbath, but what were they planning?

Have you marked the five oppositions of this unit in your Bible? The five oppositions concern (1) forgiving sins, (2) eating with tax collectors, (3) feasting and not fasting, (4) plucking grain on the Sabbath, and (5) healing on the Sabbath.
To what extent has the opposition grown?

Today's challenge:
What critical attitudes do you find in your heart?
In what ways did the Pharisees box themselves in with laws? Have you boxed someone (perhaps yourself) in by negative patterns? Pray for insight and understanding so you will not go through another day of opposing what God wants to do in your life!

Write today's challenge as a prayer:

Other prayers:

Questions for discussion or reflection:
What "withered hand" does Jesus need to deal with in your life? In your family? In your congregation?

LESSON 21

Dearest Jesus, thank you for your life. You were so loving, so calm, so organized, so sure of handling interruptions and challenges, yet you were no stranger to pain and disappointment. It's hard for me to forgive myself for not accomplishing each day's demands. It seems I often squander the moment. Only afterward do I know what I should have done or said. Does this happen because I'm not connected with you all day? It seems I'm with you for a while in the morning; then I'm off and running by myself. Let me pause and pray for wisdom every time I answer the telephone or tackle a new task. Let me pray for discernment as I listen to and interact with each person who crosses my path.

Jesus, help me to live in forgiveness today. Help me to relish the truth that you never leave me. Help me to desire your will. Amen.

Bible verse: "Whoever does the will of God is my brother and sister and mother." Mark 3:35
Are you also reviewing Mark 10:45; 1:41; and 2:9b?

Division 2: Proclamation, Mark 1:14—8:30
Unit 4: Growing Organization, Mark 3:7-35
Paragraph 1: Withdrawal, Mark 3:7-12

At first Jesus' ministry is one of growing popularity, but then growing opposition comes. A crisis develops and the enemies begin to plot Jesus' death. So Jesus uses the opposition as a stepping stone to advance his kingdom. He withdraws to the sea with a twofold purpose: to train his disciples and to make good use of the days remaining to teach this new beginning—the gospel. Watch his growing organization!

Read Mark 3:7-12 and record five observations about how Jesus changes the focus of his ministry. Refer to the map on page 240.
    Visualize the scene. Imagine yourself in the crowds as Jesus teaches! Imagine being surrounded by the sick, the lame, the demon possessed. From where did the crowds come?
    Refer to a Bible dictionary or atlas and find descriptions of the areas from which the crowds had come.

How far had people traveled to see Jesus?
Underline the following verbs.
Crush
Pressed
Fell down
Shouted
Touch
Ordered
What picture do these verbs give you?
What a magnet Jesus was! He was clearly the hero of the hour.
For what reasons did the crowd follow Jesus?
Why did Jesus give such definite orders to his disciples?
Why were the demons compelled to reveal Jesus' identity?
Why did Jesus silence them?

Today's challenge:
If the Holy Spirit reminds you to thank Jesus for his power and majesty, do it! Don't put it off until later!
Do you ever examine the organization or lack of it in your day?
Make a list of your priorities. Are you proud of them?

Write today's challenge as a prayer:

Other prayers:

Questions for discussion or reflection:
For what reason do you follow Jesus?
Does just knowing about Jesus bring salvation?
How do we receive salvation?

LESSON 22

Breathe slowly and deeply as you prepare to review the prayer and Bible verse from Lesson 21.

Division 2: Proclamation, Mark 1:14—8:30
Unit 4: Growing Organization, Mark 3:7-35
Paragraph 2: The Twelve, Mark 3:13-19a

Read verses 13-19a and record five observations. Notice that Jesus called those he wanted and that they, feeling the heartbeat of his work, came to him. What a tremendous task it was to select his disciples. It is significant that Christianity began with a group.
Why did Jesus choose twelve? (Matt. 19:28)
What three things were the disciples' responsibility?

It's easy to name the disciples if you use association. Who is always named first, fifth, ninth? See Mark 3:16-19, Matt. 10:1-4, Luke 6:14-16, and Acts 1:13.

1. Peter	5. Philip	9. James
2. James	6. Bartholomew	10. Thaddaeus
3. John	7. Matthew	11. Simon
4. Andrew	8. Thomas	12. Judas

Why did Jesus choose such ordinary men to be his disciples?
Can you name two or three characteristics of his disciples?

Today's challenge:
If you had been there, would you have wanted to be called as one of the twelve? How do your neighbors know that you are one of his disciples?
Do you care enough to reach out to your neighbors in their joys and sorrows?

Write today's challenge as a prayer:

Other prayers:

Questions for discussion or reflection:
What does "to be with him" mean to you?
Does the idea of obeying and following Jesus frighten you?
Where have you been sent out to preach? Be specific.
What exciting directions have you received from the Holy Spirit?

LESSON 23

Be still. Focus your mind and heart on Jesus as you review the prayer and Bible verse from Lesson 21.

Division 2: Proclamation, Mark 1:14—8:30
Unit 4: Growing Organization, Mark 3:7-35
Paragraph 3: Head-On Collision, Mark 3:19b-27

Read verses 19b-27 and record five observations about Jesus' confrontation against evil.

Some time has elapsed since the last paragraph. Evidently Jesus and his disciples had walked a long way and needed to rest and eat, but the crowd would not let them.

What words reveal Jesus' popularity?

Why did some say that Jesus was "out of his mind"?

What is the scribes' ridiculous accusation?

To understand the full significance of the scribes' words, read Matt. 12:23.

Why were the teachers of law so perturbed and jealous?

What was Jesus' first reasoning statement to the scribes?

What three examples did Jesus use to illustrate his point?

Notice the *ifs!*

How did Jesus prove his point with the image of the strong man?

Today's challenge:

What have you learned by watching the two great forces of good and evil at work?

In what ways do we allow the evil in our communities to take over?

Write today's challenge as a prayer:

Other prayers:

Questions for discussion or reflection:

Identify the evil forces at work in your community.

Are you involved in confronting that evil?

Does doing nothing give our tacit approval of evil?

LESSON 24

Prepare your heart for this lesson by reviewing the prayer and Bible verses from Lesson 21. Keep reviewing Mark 10:45; 1:41; and 2:9b.

Division 2: Proclamation, Mark 1:14—8:30
Unit 4: Growing Organization, Mark 3:7-35
Paragraph 4: The Unpardonable Sin, Mark 3:28-30

Study verses 28-30 and record five observations about forgiveness and blasphemy. Refer to a Bible dictionary to find out what *truly* means. Why did Jesus use *truly* here?

What sins are forgiven? (1 John 1:9)

What is blasphemy? Check a Bible dictionary if you aren't sure.

Whom can one blaspheme against and receive forgiveness?

Whom can one not blaspheme against and receive forgiveness?

How do you know you haven't committed the unpardonable sin?

What did the scribes really say the Holy Spirit was in verse 30?

Today's challenge:
Write three sentences describing the Holy Spirit.

How is the Holy Spirit a comforter to you?

Write today's challenge as a prayer:

Other prayers:

Questions for discussion or reflection:
What is the work of the Holy Spirit in our lives? In our church? See Luke 10:16.

How do we grieve, quench, reject the Holy Spirit? See Eph. 4:30-32 Thess. 5:16-19, and Luke 10:16.

When is the Holy Spirit grieved with you?

LESSON 25

Thoughtfully, review the prayer and Bible verse from Lesson 21.

Division 2: Proclamation, Mark 1:14—8:30
Unit 4: Growing Organization, Mark 3:7-35
Paragraph 5: Family of God, Mark 3:31-35

Study verses 31-35 and record five observations about whom Jesus claims as his family.

What do you think Jesus wanted to accomplish in this paragraph?

Who was bothering Jesus now?

Record the three verbs used to describe his relatives' actions.

What were Jesus' relatives worried about? How did their inquiry disturb the crowd?

Why was this a painful situation for Jesus?

Who were Jesus' brothers and sisters? (Mark 6:3, Matt. 13:55)

What is Jesus' beautiful response?

Notice the contrast between this paragraph and the previous one.

What is the important word in your memory verse?

Today's challenge:

Do we live by our emotions or will?

How can we know God's will?

If we live in God's will, we become Jesus' dearest relative!

Write today's challenge as a prayer:

Other prayers:

Questions for discussion or reflection:

What comes first in a Christian's life—feelings, faith, or will? Why? Do you live by your emotions or will? Why?

How can you relate to Jesus in this cold, impersonal, computerized world?

LESSON 26

I want to be teachable, Lord. Is there something you want to show me, some attitude you want changed, some weed of bitterness I need to pull up before you can answer my prayer? Give me a spirit of wisdom and enlighten the eyes of my heart (Eph. 1:17-18) so that I can really hear what the Holy Spirit is saying to me. I go into this study expecting to see great things!

Bible verse: "Pay attention to what you hear; the measure you give will be the measure you get, and still more will be given you." Mark 4:24

Division 2: Proclamation, Mark 1:14—8:30
Unit 5: Parables, Mark 4:1-34
Paragraph 1: Receptivity of the Word, Mark 4:1-9

Now Jesus begins to explain his mission! Jesus continues the disciples' training by teaching in parables. Parables are stories that use familiar scenes or objects to portray spiritual lessons. A parable generally has one main point and, because it is in a story form, it is usually retained longer than a statement. Through parables, Jesus takes the known and compares it with the unknown (the Kingdom of God). Try to grasp the beauty and profound truths of this unit.

Study Mark 4:1-9 and record five observations.
Who has told you the most exciting stories?
How did he or she identify with things or persons familiar to you?
How is Jesus making God's truth exciting to his listeners?
What does the word *again* tell you about this scene?
Record the details of this picturesque scene.
What is implied in Jesus' first word?

Check a Bible dictionary to find out how seed was planted in Palestine.
In one word, what is the parable about?
What does the soil represent?
Write down in your notebook the four types of soil and the fate of the seed in each.
Notice the name of this paragraph.
What does the receptivity of the Word depend on?
When do people really have ears to hear?

Today's challenge:
Is there anything the Holy Spirit is telling you that you haven't wanted to hear? Are you starving your spiritual life by materialism, busyness, television, pride, alcohol, some other compulsion?

Write today's challenge as a prayer:

Other prayers:

Questions for discussion or reflection:
What is your "soil" like on Sunday mornings? On weekdays? When you watch TV? When you shop? When you work? When you play? Think

48

about your answers! Why is the kingdom of God a mystery? Does grasping the kingdom of God require a simple or a great intellect?

LESSON 27

In stillness before God, review the prayer and meditate on the Bible verse from Lesson 26.

Division 2: Proclamation, Mark 1:14—8:30
Unit 5: Parables, Mark 4:1-34
Paragraph 2: Secret of the Kingdom, Mark 4:10-12
Paragraph 3: The Explanation, Mark 4:13-20

Study verses 10-20 and record five observations.
To whom did Jesus explain the parables?
Why didn't he explain them to the whole crowd?
The kingdom of God is a mystery. Can you explain the mystery of verse 12?

Imagine the sun shining down on a lump of wax and on a lump of wet clay. After several hours, what will be the result? The wax will have softened and become pliable; the clay will have become harder. In a similar way, we permit the Holy Spirit to soften or harden our lives. As you read Jesus' explanation of his parables, can you see unbelieving people turning hard like the clay and believers becoming more pliable?
What growth and hindrances do you see in the soil on the path? On the rocky ground? Among the thorns? In the good soil?
What is the significance of thirty-, sixty-, and a hundredfold? (Check the memory verse.)
What hinders a person's understanding?
Can you envision these four types of soil in today's society? Give examples.

Today's challenge:
What a wonderful explanation of our lives! How does this parable illustrate the preaching of the gospel?

What is your response on a Sunday morning or as you study the Word?
What kind of soil are you?
When were you most receptive and most fertile to God's Word?

Write today's challenge as a prayer:

Other prayers:

Questions for discussion or reflection:
What kind of "hearing" is evidenced in your life lately?
Do you respond readily to God's Word in some areas but resist it in others? Write down your areas of response and resistance. Be specific.
Can you see something of yourself in all four types of soil?
What did you learn about evangelism from these examples of soil?
How do your friends hear and respond to the Word?

LESSON 28

Discover that God *is* God! Review the prayer and Bible verse from Lesson 26.

Division 2: Proclamation, Mark 1:14—8:30
Unit 5: Parables, Mark 4:1-34
Paragraph 4: Use of the Word, Mark 4:21-25

Study verses 21-25 and record five observations about hearing, seeing, and receiving.
What object is used in this parable?
What does a lamp do?
What humorous image did Jesus use to make his point?
How are our lamps lighted?
As we obey our Bible verse, what happens to our light?
What is the name of the paragraph?
What is the name of the parable in Mark 4:1-9?
God loves to give his children insight.
How do people receive a full measure of light or understanding?
Is God's light helping the people around you?

Today's challenge:
When in your life did you or will you give a full measure? How much light do you shed—that of a 20-, 60- 100-, or 200-watt bulb? Why do you receive so much when you give (verse 24)?

Write today's challenge as a prayer:

Other prayers:

Questions for discussion or reflection:
What makes your light cloudy, smoky?
Why is obedience so important to grasp the grace and power of these verses?
Do you know some people who are given more and more?

LESSON 29

Be still and pray the prayer from Lesson 26. Is the Bible verse becoming more meaningful to you? What measures are you receiving?

Division 2: Proclamation, Mark 1:14—8:30
Unit 5: Parables, Mark 4:1-34
Paragraph 5: Growth of the Word, Mark 4:26-29

Study verses 26-29 and record five observations. Remember, the last paragraphs were to the hearers of the Word; this one is to the pro claimers of the Word.
What is Jesus talking about? (Look at the name of the paragraph.)
What did someone scatter on the ground?
Then what did the person do?
Meanwhile, what did the seed do?
What are three progressive developments in this parable?
What causes your progress to grow and multiply?
How is this parable like a Christian who faithfully proclaims the message of salvation in word and deed?
What must be the attitude of our hearts and minds when we teach the Word?

In whose hands is the harvest?

Today's challenge:
Why is this parable so difficult to live out in church?
What in the kingdom are you most like? A dry seed? A sprouting seed?
A plant choked by thorns? A mature plant producing thirty-, sixty-, or
a hundredfold? Or are you burned out?

Write today's challenge as a prayer:

Other prayers:

Questions for discussion or reflection:
How does this parable give you hope when you are discouraged with
your life, family, church, or work?
Are you letting the seed grow or are you nagging, correcting, and
advising? (Isa. 42:3)
Whom do you know who is like a blade, an unripe ear, a full head of
grain? Can you give some examples? Take some time to meditate on
the joyful reaping!

LESSON 30

Praise. Pray a song! How's your hearing as you review the prayer and
Bible verse from Lesson 26?

Division 2: Proclamation, Mark 1:14—8:30
Unit 5: Parables, Mark 4:1-34
Paragraph 6: Power of the Word, Mark 4:30-32

Study verses 30-32 and record five observations. Focus on what is said
about the kingdom of God. What a lesson! Jesus wanted to teach the
disciples another aspect of the kingdom of God, so he asked a pointed
question. You can imagine how the disciples waited for some great
revelation of truth!

To what did Jesus compare the kingdom of God?

Do you think his comparison surprised the disciples?
How big is a mustard seed?
What has to be done with the seed so it can be of use?
What does the mustard seed represent?
What are the characteristics of a mustard seed?
What do the branches and the birds represent in this parable?

Today's challenge:
What tremendous hope does this parable give the disciples and us?
What small beginnings have you or others made that might, with God's power, lead to great outcomes?

Write today's challenge as a prayer:

Other prayers:

Questions for discussion or reflection:
How do you see the truths of these four parables at work in your church?
How do all four parables reveal the kingdom of God?
What evidence have you seen of the power of the Word? Be specific.

LESSON 31

Be still! Pray the prayer from Lesson 26. Review all the memorized verses.

Division 2: Proclamation, Mark 1:14—8:30
Unit 5: Parables, Mark 4:1-34
Paragraph 7: Many Parables, Mark 4:33-34

Study verses 33-34 and record five observations.
Why didn't Mark record all the parables of Jesus?
How much will Jesus allow a person to learn?
What does that mean?
Have you studied and memorized the Bible verse for Unit 5?

What do the parables mean to you now?
Why did Jesus speak to the crowd only in parables?
Why did he give his disciples more instruction?

Today's challenge:
Review and study the choice of parables Mark recorded. What a tremendous vision Mark had, guided by the Holy Spirit! Close your eyes and meditate on how you heard the Word last Sunday and today in your daily devotions.

Write today's challenge as a prayer:

Other prayers:

Questions for discussion or reflection:
Have you tried to teach in parables, taking the known around you and applying it to life?
Write a short parable about a familiar object in your home and apply it to life.

LESSON 32

Heavenly Father, I stand amazed at how clearly and directly Jesus prayed. He stilled storms in people's lives, healed all manner of sickness, and even used his authority over demons and death. I know I must become like a child and make my needs known to you specifically and openly, not in generalities. I need to be able to accept your grace and see the answers to my prayers. But I fear I'm too lazy and scared to work at it.

It's so easy to say "bless this, bless that," instead of "give me love, and help me to remember I don't need the luxury of having things my way!" Holy Spirit, help me just for today to ask definitely, to relinquish my prayer to you, and to keep alert to the answer. Help me to see your miracles splashed all around and to enjoy them with others. Thank you! Amen.

Bible verse: "Go home to your friends, and tell them how much the

Lord has done for you, and what mercy he has shown on you." Mark 5:19

Division 2: Proclamation, Mark 1:14—8:30
Unit 6: Miracles, Mark 4:35—5:43
Paragraph 1: Power over Nature, Mark 4:35-41

Study verses 35-41 and record five observations.
   We are living in an age that stresses the visual sense. What profound lessons Jesus taught through visual means. In the previous paragraph, Jesus has been teaching verbally, but now his visual portrayals of power are stressed. Hence, we start a new unit, Miracles. Try to visualize each scene as if it were taking place before your eyes.

The long day of teaching was over!
Where were the disciples (4:1) and what time of day was it?
What do you think "just as he was" means?
Is it likely that many of the disciples had faced storms like this before?
Describe the most frightening storm you have experienced.
When have you reacted like the disciples when storms arise?
Why did Jesus seem unconcerned when the storm arose?
What three action verbs describe how Jesus calmed the storm?
How did Jesus challenge the disciples?
When did you last stand awestruck at Jesus' power?
Over what did Jesus teach his disciples that he has power?

Today's challenge:
Storms come in other forms too.
What are some storms in your life?
How do you react when Jesus seems to be asleep?
When last did you become involved in a friend's hurt or storm?

Write today's challenge as a prayer:

Other prayers:

Questions for discussion or reflection:
Do Christians have "smoother sailing" than non-Christians?
When faced with a storm, do you panic or trust?
Is your church concerned about those in rough waters—for that family

with an alcoholic, the separated parent, the lonesome elderly, the bewildered teenager, the shunned minority, the jobless man or woman, or the man or woman in prison?

LESSON 33

Review the prayer and Bible verse from Lesson 32. Are you telling others? In order to grow, one must speak the Word (Rom. 10:10).

Division 2: Proclamation, Mark 1:14—8:30
Unit 6: Miracles, Mark 4:35—5:43
Paragraph 2: Power over Demons, Mark 5:1-13

Study verses 1-13 and record five observations. Focus on the visual and emotional intensity of this miracle. What a picture of evil and terror versus power and majesty!
Where is the country of Gerasenes?

Please read this paragraph out loud, stressing the verbs and substituting *this man* for the pronouns that refer to him. Visualize the scene.
Where did this man live?
What had the demons done to the man?
What new information do you learn about demons?
Who spoke to Jesus, the man or the demon?
Why did Jesus ask the demon's name?
Why did the demons ask Jesus to send them into the herd of pigs? (Luke 8:31)
How would you have felt if you had witnessed this scene?
Over what has Jesus now demonstrated his power?

Today's challenge:
Does this miracle fill you with faith or fear?
Are you curious about the occult, the New Age movement, Ouija boards, astrology, or the many demonic forces that are so prevalent today? Why are they dangerous?

Write today's challenge as a prayer:

Other prayers:

Questions for discussion or reflection:
How do demons destroy our relationships with each other and God?
How powerful are demonic forces and the occult in your locality?

LESSON 34

Pray the prayer and review the Bible verse from Lesson 32.

Division 2: Proclamation, Mark 1:14—8:30
Unit 6: Miracles, Mark 4:35—5:43
Paragraph 3: The Departure, Mark 5:14-20

Study verses 14-20 and record five observations.
Why did the herdsmen flee?
What astonishing miracle did the people find?
Compare the demoniac before and after. Use the words of Scripture.
Why didn't the people have any trouble getting rid of Jesus?
What was the healed man's request?
What did Jesus ask him to do? Why?
How do you imagine his family responded to him?
Where is Decapolis?
Were the people afraid of Jesus' supernatural power or afraid to give up their security?

Today's challenge:
When have you wished Jesus' way of life would not be so serious?
Do you just stand by and watch what is happening in your country's politics, your neighborhood, your church, or do you get involved?
When did you last marvel at what Jesus does? Are there some "swine" in your life that you love more than Jesus?

Write today's challenge as a prayer:

Other prayers:

Questions for discussion or reflection:
Name some of the evils in our society that we are afraid to touch. Why?
What in our lives do we wish Jesus wouldn't touch?
Can you grasp what Jesus asked of the demoniac so that he could have a new beginning?

LESSON 35

Pray the prayer and review the Bible verse from Lesson 32.

Division 2: Proclamation, Mark 1:14—8:30
Unit 6: Miracles, Mark 4:35—5:43
Paragraph 4: Jairus, Mark 5:21-24a

Study verses 21-24a and record five observations.
Where was Jesus and who met him?
What does Scripture tell us about Jairus?
How did Jairus humbly face the storm in his life?
What two things did he ask of Jesus?
How was Jesus living the key verse?

Today's challenge:
Notice how Jesus handled the pressures of the day! Notice the last line, "So he went with him." Jesus does the same with us!
What definite concern or frustration do you need to put into Jesus' hands? This is the opportune time.
How can you pray for understanding and wisdom in order to make your prayer definite, simple, and exciting?
Make a list of these definite prayers.

Write today's challenge as a prayer:

Other prayers:

Questions for discussion or reflection:
When facing a storm, what steps do you take?
How do you allow your faith to overcome your fears?
Are there places you wouldn't want Jesus to come with you?

LESSON 36

Relax before God in quietness. Pray the prayer and review the Bible verse from Lesson 32.

Division 2: Proclamation, Mark 1:14—8:30
Unit 6: Miracles, Mark 4:35—5:43
Paragraph 5: Power over Sickness, Mark 5:24b-34

Study verses 24b-34 and record five observations about faith and healing.
Where was Jesus going?
Did the woman with a great physical need have a right to be in the crowd and touch Jesus? (Lev. 15:19-30)
What six things do you learn about this woman? Write them in your notebook.
How did the woman hear about Jesus?
How was this woman trying to increase her courage?
Notice her words. How important was it that she touched Jesus?
Why did Jesus make her reveal herself?
How did Jesus strengthen her faith?
Who was impatiently waiting for Jesus to move on?
What has Jesus now demonstrated power over?

Today's challenge:
Touching Jesus' garment while full of expectation is identified as an act of faith. Does this incident awaken faith in you?

In what ways can we reach out and touch Jesus?
How much do we use touch in our families?
Think about how much joy Jesus brought to this woman. Is the Christian life measured by the joy one brings to others?

Write today's challenge as a prayer:

Other prayers:

Questions for discussion or reflection:
How can we help each other in our storms of life?
Is it easier to stand and criticize or become involved?
Could Jesus have said Mark 5:34 to you?

LESSON 37

Rest in the truth that God dwells within you. Pray the prayer and review the Bible verse from Lesson 32.

Division 2: Proclamation, Mark 1:14—8:30
Unit 6: Miracles, Mark 4:35—5:43
Paragraph 6: Power over Death, Mark 5:35-43

Study verses 35-43 and record five observations. How encouraged Jairus must have been when he watched the healing of the woman! What do you think happened to Jairus's faith when he heard the message from his house?
What was Jesus' response, his word of comfort?
Why did Jesus only allow three disciples to join him?
What had already begun at the house?
How many people entered the sickroom with Jesus?
Visualize the scene in the sickroom. What two things did Jesus do? (verse 41)
How did the parents react to the healing of their daughter?
Why did Jesus give such strict commands? Notice the tender reminder that immediately followed.

What has Jesus now demonstrated his power over?

Today's challenge:
How do you identify with loved ones who suffer from illness, depression, low self-esteem, unbalanced emotions, or tangled relationships? Be specific!

Write today's challenge as a prayer:

Other prayers:

Questions for discussion or reflection:
When have you been like Jairus? Like the servant from the ruler's house? Like the mourners? Like the disciples? Like the exuberant family?

LESSON 38

Dear Jesus, in these lessons you led the disciples through their internship. How I thank you for your love and grace. You never give up on them, or on me! Help me today to choose to live above my stressful circumstances and put my self-pity, low self-esteem, sensitive spirit, pride, and worldly ignorance into your hands as I study and pray. May your Word, which is living and active, sharper than any two-edged sword (Heb. 4:12), give me spiritual discipline, as well as abundant joy! Help me to take heart in this evil world and to have no fear. Assure me of the presence of your ministering angels around the ones I love. Thank you, Father.

Bible verse: "Take heart, it is I; do not be afraid." Mark 6:50b

Division 2: Proclamation, Mark 1:14—8:30
Unit 7: Internship, Mark 6:1-56
Paragraph 1: Nazareth, Mark 6:1-6a

Jesus has taught his disciples by example and by verbal and visual means. Now he puts them through a period of internship. They have crucial lessons to learn. They need a deeper knowledge of God and a stronger faith in his omnipotent power so that they do not fall in with the false religious leaders of that day.

Study Mark 6:1-6a and record five observations about Jesus' reception in his own town.

Notice the questions the people asked about Jesus. Take into account all the miracles Jesus had just performed. What gifts did the people admit Jesus had?

These people couldn't accept Jesus, the man they had known as a carpenter, as the Messiah.
How had they expected the Messiah to come?
Who did many people say Jesus was?
In the previous paragraph, Jesus had marveled at Jairus's faith.
What did he marvel at here? (See also Luke 4:28-30.)

Today's challenge:
In what ways is Jesus' work in your life limited as it was in Nazareth?
Do we take offense at people excited about Jesus?
Why is it dangerous to look on Jesus as a mere man, a marvelous historical figure?
How do jealousy, prejudice, and familiarity blind our eyes to Jesus' power in our lives and the fellowship we could have with others? Give examples from your daily life.

Write today's challenge as a prayer:

Other prayers:

Questions for discussion or reflection:
Do you see Jesus for who he is and what he can do, or is he limited to being a great man in your mind?
Does a person need to be respected or honored to be used by God?
How do we limit Jesus' power in our homes, community, and church?

LESSON 39

Praise the Lord! Pray the prayer and review the Bible verse from Lesson 38. Notice the verbs!

Division 2: Proclamation, Mark 1:14—8:30
Unit 7: Internship, Mark 6:1-56
Paragraph 2: Two by Two, Mark 6:6b-13

Study verses 6b-13 and record five observations about the disciples' internship. Having been rejected in Nazareth, Jesus walked to other villages. Imagine the joy and excitement of the people in those villages!

The disciples then were about to experience the great joy of practicing what they had been learning.

Why did Jesus send them two by two?

Why did Jesus give them the power over unclean spirits?

Make a list of his practical orders in your notebook.

Why did he give them such detailed instructions?

Why were they to "shake off the dust" when they were not welcomed?

What message did they preach?

Who else started with this message? (Mark 1:4, 14-15)

Today's challenge:
When last did you hear a sermon on repentance?
How are you making use of the power that Jesus gave to the disciples?

Write today's challenge as a prayer:

Other prayers:

Questions for discussion or reflection:
What specific instructions has Jesus given you?
Are you responsible for others accepting Christ?
What part is our responsibility? What part is God's?

LESSON 40

Be still. Pray the prayer and review the Bible verse from Lesson 38. Has the Bible verse become a part of your life?

Division 2: Proclamation, Mark 1:14—8:30
Unit 7: Internship, Mark 6:1-56
Paragraph 3: Who Is Jesus? Mark 6:14-16
Paragraph 4: Herod, Mark 6:17-29

Study verses 14-29 and record five observations. Yes, Jesus and his disciples were becoming known.
Whose startled conscience was awakening? Why?
What three reports were circulating about Jesus' identity?
What religious cults and sects today consider Jesus to be a mere man?
Why do you think Herod granted such a rash request?
Why didn't Herod kill John immediately after his arrest?
What two great forces do we encounter in this paragraph?
What one act of mercy do you find in this paragraph?

Today's challenge:
Are you dominated by the power of a recognizable sin in your life?
Are you afraid to take up acts of mercy?
John gave his life for God's kingdom. How do you think he would respond to the preachers today who say that if you invite Christ into your life everything will be just fine?

Write today's challenge as a prayer:

Other prayers:

Questions for discussion or reflection:
Who is Jesus in your life? In your family?
What power is Jesus in your church?
Do you "bind up the brokenhearted" or kill by gossip? (Isa. 61:1)
If you live and preach Christ, do your problems increase or decrease?

LESSON 41

Have a time of quiet praise. Pray the prayer and review the Bible verse from Lesson 38.

Division 2: Proclamation, Mark 1:14—8:30
Unit 7: Internship, Mark 6:1-56
Paragraph 5: Feeding the Five Thousand, Mark 6:30-44

Study verses 30-44 and record five observations. The disciples were returning from their first internship assignment.
What reveals the disciples' eagerness and enthusiasm?
What were the disciples now called?
Why did Jesus suggest an undisturbed conference?
Where did they plan to go?
What did the people do?
Why did Jesus have compassion on the people?
What was the mood of the disciples as they faced the impossible task of feeding the people?
Why couldn't they buy enough bread to feed everyone?
How did Jesus handle the change in plans?
What resources did Jesus have to accomplish his task?
Record the details of the actual feeding. Mark may have reported what Peter had seen and described.
What reverence for food and orderliness do you notice in the way Jesus handled the feeding?
What does this miracle tell us about Jesus?

Today's challenge:
How do you face upset plans and interruptions in your daily life? Do you view them as an opportunity to see God work? How do you face the millions who are starving today?

Write today's challenge as a prayer:

Other prayers:

Questions for discussion or reflection:
In what ways are we wallowing in the impossible so we can't see the possible?
How does Jesus want to feed us spiritually?
How are we listening together in prayer?
Are we facing the facts and making use of the resources at hand?

LESSON 42

In stillness before God, pray the prayer and review the Bible verse from Lesson 38. Have you memorized the verse yet?

Division 2: Proclamation, Mark 1:14—8:30
Unit 7: Internship, Mark 6:1-56
Paragraph 6: Time for Quiet, Mark 6:45-46
Paragraph 7: Walking on the Sea, Mark 6:47-52

Study verses 45-52 and record five observations. Notice the words *immediately*, *made*, and *dismissed*.
What was wrong? What prompted this uncharacteristic behavior in Jesus? (John 6:15)
Where were the disciples told to go?
As before, how did Jesus get his strength when Satan tempted him?
Why do you think Jesus "intended to pass them by"?
How is Jesus trying to show his disciples who he is in this and the previous paragraph?

Today's challenge:
When have you been utterly terrified?
Apply Jesus' words in your situation.
When last have you been astounded by an answered prayer?
Are your prayers definite so there will be something to be amazed at when the answers come?

Write today's challenge as a prayer:

Other prayers:

Questions for discussion or reflection:
What winds are against you?
In what ways are you "straining at the oars"? Be specific.
Tell about a "miracle" that happened recently.

LESSON 43

Once again, pray the prayer and review the Bible verse from Lesson 38. Are you living by this verse?

Division 2: Proclamation, Mark 1:14—8:30
Unit 7: Internship, Mark 6:1-56
Paragraph 8: Gennesaret, Mark 6:53-56

Study verses 53-56 and record five observations.
Find Gennesaret on your map. Jesus' popularity continued to escalate!

Beginning with verse 54, record the verbs Mark used to describe the people's excitement.
Why did they bring the sick to marketplaces?
How many people were healed?
Can you imagine, see, and hear the joy as Jesus and his disciples traveled through the region?
Record lessons from the seven previous paragraphs that the disciples learned during their internship.

Today's challenge:
Are you bringing physically, mentally, or spiritually sick people to Jesus so that they might touch him and be healed?
When were you last excited about Jesus?

Write today's challenge as a prayer:

Other prayers:

Questions for discussion or reflection:
If Jesus walked down the aisle in your church some Sunday morning and healed people, what would you do? Doesn't he still heal people? Have you asked him to?

LESSON 44

Jesus, what hard, intensive lessons the disciples had to learn! They had to break with tradition. Are you asking me to face the difficult problems I see—the belligerent teenager who needs attention, the hurting couple that is separated or divorced, the suffering senior who longs for heaven, the wounded child in an abusive home, the friction between my own family members?

Oh, God, where do I start? Will you give me "the spirit of wisdom and understanding, the spirit of counsel and might, the spirit of knowledge and the fear of the Lord" (Isa. 11:2)? Help me meet the nitty-gritty problems of life and walk on tiptoe in expectancy of your answers. Thank you, Jesus!

Bible verse: "He has done everything well; he even makes the deaf to hear and the mute to speak." Mark 7:37
Repeat the words. What feeling envelops you?

Division 2: Proclamation, Mark 1:14—8:30
Unit 8: Intensive Training, Mark 7:1—8:30
Paragraph 1: Unwashed Hands, Mark 7:1-8

Study verses 1-8 and record five observations about obedience to God's laws.

Jesus' students had learned many lessons during their internship. Now they faced even more intensive ones as Jesus exposed the false teachings of the church leaders of the day. The disciples had to be set straight regarding traditions and teachings. Notice how clearly and concisely Jesus handled each issue.

What delegation confronted Jesus in this paragraph?

Check a Bible atlas or the map on page 240 to see how far they had traveled.

Who were the Pharisees and the scribes? (Refer to a Bible dictionary or encyclopedia if you don't know.)

Notice who the Pharisees and scribes attacked.

With what did they find fault?

What Old Testament prophet did Jesus quote to condemn their attack?

How does the prophet speak to this issue?

Did Jesus observe the levitical law?

What did Jesus' accusers view as more important than God's commandments?

Today's challenge:
How hard is it for you to break, follow, or sidestep tradition?

When we obey a human tradition, are we breaking the law of God?

What traditions would you like to see changed?

Why is the attitude of the heart so important?

Write today's challenge as a prayer:

Other prayers:

Questions for discussion or reflection:
In what ways are we hypocrites?

Do we emphasize our virtues and others' faults?

Do we attend church and give to charity in order to be seen by other people?

Do we participate in worship and public prayers while our thoughts are elsewhere?

Which of your traditions might be compared to the "tradition of the elders"?

Are some of our traditions too severe and meaningless for young Christians?

LESSON 45

Pray the prayer and review the Bible verse from Lesson 44. Read slowly and out loud. What feelings envelop you?

Division 2: Proclamation, Mark 1:14—8:30
Unit 8: Intensive Training, Mark 7:1—8:30
Paragraph 2: Corban, Mark 7:9-13

Study verses 9-13 and record five observations.
What does it mean to reject one of God's commandments?
What had these critics made more important—God's commandment or human tradition?
What is Moses' commandment? (Exod. 20:12)
What blessing is promised if one obeys the fourth commandment?
What is "corban"?
How did the Pharisees use God as an excuse for not helping their parents?
What effect did their tradition have on the Word of God?
Do you think the Pharisees and scribes gave God what they refused to share with their parents?

Today's challenge:
How do you judge whether or not a person is growing spiritually?
How have your beliefs had to change?
Read verses 9 and 13 again. Has Christmas, Easter, Thanksgiving, or another holiday become a disgruntled tradition in your life?
In what ways do you make God's Word void?
Is yours a problem of sincere, but misdirected, religious zeal?

Write today's challenge as a prayer:

Other prayers:

Questions for discussion or reflection:
Are you too set in your ways of doing things? If so, how?
Do you have to possess the luxury of being right?
In what ways could you be wrong according to Scripture?

LESSON 46

Relax. Pray the prayer and review the Bible verse from Lesson 44.

Division 2: Proclamation, Mark 1:14—8:30
Unit 8: Intensive Training, Mark 7:1—8:30
Paragraph 3: Listen, Mark 7:14-16
Paragraph 4: Within and Without, Mark 7:17-23

Study verses 14-23 and record five observations about defilement.
What a challenge! What a breach between Jesus and the religious leaders of the day!
Whom did Jesus want to hear this lesson?
How do we know this is an important lesson?
What did "defile" mean to the Pharisees and to Jesus?
Why was Jesus' statement in verse 15 such a bombshell?
(See Leviticus 11.)
What foods did Jesus declare clean?
Old, fixed ideas are hard to shake. What defilement did Jesus say comes from the heart? List twelve of them in your notebook.
What great truth about human nature was Jesus proclaiming?

Today's challenge:
Where do you see yourself in the list of defilements? (verses 21-22)
Which of the evils shackle you most?

Write today's challenge as a prayer:

Other prayers:

Questions for discussion or reflection:
What do you do when your evil heart wins?
What impact does your social environment have on you?
What impact does your home have on you?
Is there a spiritual vacuum within you?

LESSON 47

Pray the prayer and review the Bible verse from Lesson 44.

Division 2: Proclamation, Mark 1:14—8:30
Unit 8: Intensive Training, Mark 7:1—8:30
Paragraph 5: Gentile Woman, Mark 7:24-30

Study verses 24-30 and record five observations about the Gentile woman. Imagine what Jesus talked about with his disciples on these long walks through Palestine.
Why did Jesus withdraw from the populous centers?
Locate Tyre and Sidon on a map. Jesus was in Gentile territory.
What do you discover about this woman?
How do you think she heard about Jesus?
Who are the "children"?
Who were the "dogs"?
What are the "crumbs"?
What statement of Jesus is a play on words?
What was the woman willing to be to receive a blessing?
Why did Jesus commend the woman for her faith?
How great is Jesus' power over demons?
How fully did the woman trust Jesus?

Today's challenge:
Think of the woman's effort, understanding, and priority!
What intensive lesson did the disciples have to learn?
What is your priority for your family members?

Write today's challenge as a prayer:

Other prayers:

Questions for discussion or reflection:
Are you being an extension of Jesus to the "Greek people" around you?

Whom are you nudging in the right direction?
When you face trials do you look for Jesus' love and kindness in the trial?

LESSON 48

Pray the prayer and review the Bible verse from Lesson 44. Think about what Jesus has done for you.

Division 2: Proclamation, Mark 1:14—8:30
Unit 8: Intensive Training, Mark 7:1—8:30
Paragraph 6: Be Opened, Mark 7:31-37

Study verses 31-37 and record five observations about this amazing healing. Trace Jesus' journey.
Whom had he already healed in the Decapolis? (Mark 5:1-20)
What evidence is there that the man called Legion had been an effective evangelist?
  Imagine the disciples' astonishment as the healed man began to speak. Could the gospel really have such power? What had been wrong with the man they brought to Jesus?
  Oh, the beauty of Jesus. How he could identify with each one! Notice the sign language he used as he healed the man. Give reasons for each step in the healing.
1. Took him aside
2. Put fingers in his ears
3. Spat and touched his tongue
4. Looked up to heaven
5. Sighed
6. Said to him, "Be opened"
What was to be opened?
What were the results? Find three things.

Today's challenge:
Of all the miracles performed in the Decapolis, Mark selected this one. The One promised by Isaiah had come alive (Isa. 35:5-6)! Can this

deafness and speech problem be applied to you and me in a spiritual sense? Are there those who cannot hear in our midst?

Write today's challenge as a prayer:

Other prayers:

Questions for discussion or reflection:
How do we find ourselves helping the "deaf people" in our communities, place of work, church, and home? Notice how deliberate Jesus is. Are we willing to see the stalk, then the head, and then the full head of grain (Mark 4:26-29) according to God's grace?

LESSON 49

Pray aloud the prayer and recite the Bible verse from Lesson 44.

Division 2: Proclamation, Mark 1:14—8:30
Unit 8: Intensive Training, Mark 7:1—8:30
Paragraph 7: Feeding the Four Thousand, Mark 8:1-10

Study verses 1-10 and record five observations. Notice how Mark began this chapter: "In those days when there was again."
What was he trying to show his readers?
How long had the people been with Jesus?
How far had some of them come?
Why did Jesus feed the four thousand?
Compare the disciples' attitude here with their attitude at the feeding of the five thousand (Mark 6:37). What differences do you see?
How did Jesus cut through the disciples' negativity?
Notice Jesus' organization in feeding the four thousand. Record the ten steps in your notebook.
Contrast the feeding of the four thousand with the feeding of the five thousand (Mark 6:30-44).

What differences do you see?
Where did Jesus take the disciples afterward?

Today's challenge:
Just for today, repeat the Bible verse many times. Are you deaf to the aching hearts and troubled lives of those around you?
What bread of life could you share with yourself and others today?

Write today's challenge as a prayer:

Other prayers:

Questions for discussion or reflection:
Do you have troubles and joys that are too small to talk to God about? (See Matt. 6:31-32.)
Are you so busy or worried that you don't take time to express your distress in words, or your joys in praise?
Have you ever been burdened with something and felt the Holy Spirit remind you, "Tell it to Jesus." Did you?

LESSON 50

Be still before God as you pray the prayer and review the Bible verse from Lesson 44.

Division 2: Proclamation, Mark 1:14—8:30
Unit 8: Intensive Training, Mark 7:1—8:30
Paragraph 8: Request for a Sign, Mark 8:11-13

Study verses 11-13 and record five observations about Jesus' priorities.
As soon as Jesus arrived on the west side of the sea, who was waiting to attack him?
Why was their request for a sign ridiculous?
Why did Jesus sigh?
How would the Pharisees have responded if Jesus had given the sign they sought?

Who is the biggest sign from heaven?
Did Jesus ever perform miracles just to show he could?
What intensive training did the disciples receive here?
Check the map on page 240 to determine where they sailed to next.

Today's challenge:
Just for today, trust Jesus with your individual needs. Anytime the need bothers you, whisper, "I give it to you, Jesus."
Is it wrong to seek signs?
Have you ever prayed, asking for a sign?

Write today's challenge as a prayer:

Other prayers:

Questions for discussion or reflection:
What signs or revelations has the Lord given you? Be specific.
Are you sometimes so materialistically minded that you don't see the miracle around you?
Are you in some ways spiritually blind, like the Pharisees?

LESSON 51

Pray the prayer and review the Bible verse from Lesson 44.

Division 2: Proclamation, Mark 1:14—8:30
Unit 8: Intensive Training, Mark 7:1—8:30
Paragraph 9: Yeast of the Pharisees, Mark 8:14-21

Study verses 14-21 and record five observations about understanding spiritual truth. Notice where Jesus and his disciples were and what they were doing.
On what were the disciples focusing their eyes?
What is the yeast of the Pharisees and Herod?
Read Jesus' penetrating questions in a voice you think he would have used.

What is the hardness of heart that Jesus was concerned about?
How did Jesus expect the disciples to use their senses?
Why did Jesus have to make the disciples understand spiritual things?
Did the disciples finally understand? (Matt. 16:12)
Think of the joy the disciples must have experienced when they understood.

Today's challenge:
How many of the questions Jesus asked his disciples challenge you?
In what ways has Jesus made your heart soften? Are there any hard parts left?
Although you may have come through trials and temptations, when were you slow to believe?
When do you refuse to face yourself?

Just for today, pray for a listening ear, and receive the joy of revelation!

Write today's challenge as a prayer:

Other prayers:

Questions for discussion or reflection:
In what ways are we like the Pharisees?
What should we do in our homes or congregations when we don't perceive or understand?
How great is your praise when you do perceive spiritual truth?

LESSON 52

Pray the prayer and review the Bible verse from Lesson 44. Have you memorized it?

Division 2: Proclamation, Mark 1:14—8:30
Unit 8: Intensive Training, Mark 7:1—8:30
Paragraph 10: Restored Sight, Mark 8:22-26

Study verses 22-26 and record five observations.

Whom do you think brought the blind man to Jesus?
Why didn't Jesus fulfill their request exactly as they asked?
Turn your eyes on Jesus. Record seven things Jesus did with the blind man. Tell why Jesus acted as he did each time.
Why did Jesus heal the man's eyes so gradually?
What profound lesson does this teach us?
Why did Jesus send the healed man home?

Today's challenge:
Keep your eyes covered for one-half hour today and see what you miss most.
In what ways is your vision faulty?
Jesus will meet all our needs. What area of your life needs Jesus' touch?
What is the first step to take in seeking God's healing?

Write today's challenge as a prayer:

Other prayers:

Questions for discussion or reflection:
What lesson does Jesus teach by healing this man in stages?
What people have you seen healed gradually from physical, psychological, or spiritual ills?
How would you evaluate your spiritual vision? Nearly perfect? A little blurred? Almost blind?

LESSON 53

Have a time for quiet praise. Pray the prayer and review the Bible verse from Lesson 44.

Division 2: Proclamation, Mark 1:14—8:30
Unit 8: Intensive Training, Mark 7:1—8:30
Paragraph 11: The Great Confession, Mark 8:27-30

Study verses 27-30 and record five observations. Find Caesarea Philippi on your map.

The intensive training is over. Jesus gives his disciples the crucial test. What was his first question?

What was the disciples' three-part answer?

How often do you think the disciples had discussed this question among themselves? Who did people think Jesus was? (Mark 3:21-22; 4:41; 5:17; 6:3, 14-15)

What did these answers say about Jesus?

After they had answered him, Jesus asked the most important question. What did he ask?

Why was Peter's answer so right?

What did his answer reveal to Jesus?

Why weren't the disciples to tell anyone about Jesus at that time?

Today's challenge:

What does the Messiah mean to you?

Just for today, how can you live out Peter's answer?

We have now finished the Proclamation Division 2. Review the titles of Units 3 through 8. What intensive lessons does your review reveal?

Write today's challenge as a prayer:

Other prayers:

Questions for discussion or reflection:

Just having knowledge of Jesus is not enough. What do we need to be one of His?

Review the paragraph names and choose the intensive lesson that means the most to you. Which lesson do you think was most shocking or difficult for the disciples?

LESSON 54

Dear merciful Father, I remember how fallen leaves in the yard can dance hither and yon—first in one direction and then in the other. Is that a picture of my life because I put off or refuse to take up the cross? Am I refusing to face that problem, afraid to share that disappointment, reluctant to confess that sin to someone? Father, am

I afraid to take up the cross and follow Jesus because I'd have to cut out fault-finding and criticism? Is my business keeping me locked into my family and myself? Father, in mercy, help me to deny myself and take up the cross and follow Jesus. Amen.

Bible verse: "If any want to become my followers, let them deny themselves and take up their cross and follow me." Mark 8:34b

Division 3: Passion, Mark 8:31—16:20
Unit 9: Crisis Week, Mark 8:31—9:29
Paragraph 1: Jesus' Cross, Mark 8:31-33

We have finished the first two divisions of Jesus' life, the preparation (1:1-13) and the proclamation (1:14—8:30). Mark devoted only eight chapters to these two divisions that cover one and one-half years. In contrast, he devoted almost eight chapters to the third division, the passion, that covers the last week of Jesus' life.

The great task has been accomplished. The Servant has taught his followers many lessons, but the greatest one is this: He, the long awaited Messiah, is here! How will Jesus help his disciples grasp his passion—his dying on the cross, his work of redemption?

Study 8:31-33 and record five interesting observations.
Why did Jesus call himself the Son of Man?
Notice the name of this division. What was Jesus' passion?
Had Jesus ever mentioned his death before? (Mark 2:20)
What did Jesus prophesy the Son of Man must endure? Record five things in your notebook.
Where would these events take place? (Luke 13:33)
What body of men comprised the elders, chief priests, and scribes? Refer to a Bible encyclopedia if you're not sure.
Why did Jesus say Peter was a tool of the devil?
Notice the paragraph name. Why was Jesus so firm with Peter?
What do the words *cross* or *suffering* mean to you?
What was Jesus' cross?
Why hadn't Jesus talked about his death before?

Today's challenge:
Have you ever been in Peter's shoes?
Have you ever tried to change things that were beyond your ability to change?

Write today's challenge as a prayer:

Other prayers:

Questions for discussion or reflection:
Peter took offense at the cross. Why? How is the cross an offense today? We speak so much about the trauma of being rejected—of unfaithfulness, divorce, abuse, unemployment, or ridicule. How would Jesus handle all of these?

LESSON 55

Pray the prayer and review the Bible verse from Lesson 54. Notice the verbs.

Division 3: Passion, Mark 8:31—16:20
Unit 9: Crisis Week, Mark 8:31—9:29
Paragraph 2: The Disciples' Cross, Mark 8:34—9:1

Study the paragraph. Record five observations.
How do we know that what Jesus says here is important?
If anyone wants to follow Jesus, what three things must he or she do?
What is the difference between self-denial and denial of self?
What is the cross? Do the unconverted have a cross?
What misconceptions do we have about the cross today?
There is a warning and a promise in verse 35. What points to the cross?
As in our day, the people of Jesus' day were very money conscious. What is the reward for taking up one's cross?
What is an adulterous generation? (Matt. 16:4)
When will these people see the kingdom of God come with power? When will we?

In your notebook or on a piece of paper, draw a straight line horizontally across the page. That line is your will! Now draw a perpendicular line from God to form a cross. That is God's will for you. This

81

comes when God reaches down and says: "No, that's sin, not your will, my will." The cross comes when we permit his will to cross our will.

Today's challenge:
What does the cross mean to you?
Do we learn obedience through what we suffer?
Name some of your crosses.

Write today's challenge as a prayer:

Other prayers:

Questions for discussion or reflection:
Is your sinful self on the cross? Do we admit that we are powerless, and cannot manage our own lives?
Are we willing to see our sins—to admit to the alcoholic, the work-aholic, the food addict, and the sex addict that we have trouble with self too?
Do we think of ourselves more highly than others?
Do we find ourselves on level ground at the foot of the cross?
What is the difference between a Christian and an unconverted sinner?

LESSON 56

Pray the prayer and review the Bible verse from Lesson 54. Is it becoming more meaningful to you?

Division 3: Passion, Mark 8:31—16:20
Unit 9: Crisis Week, Mark 8:31—9:29
Paragraph 3: The Great Confirmation, Mark 9:2-8

Read verses 2-8 and record five observations.
Why did Jesus take Peter, James, and John with him?
Why did he take them up a high mountain?
Visualize the picture of Jesus with the two Old Testament personalities present. What was the significance of Moses' and Elijah's presence with Jesus at this time? (Luke 9:31)

How would you have reacted if you had been one of the three disciples?
Why did Peter want to make three dwelling tents?
What was the significance of the Father's powerful statement at this time?
Where had we heard it before?
What important phrase was added?
Did Peter and John ever speak of this event? (II Pet. 1:16-18; 1 John 1:14)

Today's challenge:
Were three disciples "transformed by the renewing of the mind" (Rom. 12:2) in the presence of Jesus? Can we be?
Does this scene prove to you that the spiritual world is powerful and real? How?
When have you grasped a bit of his glory?
In what way does this paragraph point to the cross?

Write today's challenge as a prayer:

Other prayers:

Questions for discussion or reflection:
How did the three disciples recognize Moses and Elijah?
Does this scene give us a glimpse of heaven?
Do you think we will know each other in heaven?
When can we see Jesus only?
Does Rom. 12:1-2 give us a vision?
Our culture tells us to seek everything—possessions, position, pride. How does the cross ask us to reverse our values?

LESSON 57

Be still and think about your cross. Then pray the prayer and review the Bible verse from Lesson 54.

Division 3: Passion, Mark 8:31—16:20
Unit 9: Crisis Week, Mark 8:31—9:29
Paragraph 4: The Great Prophet, Mark 9:9-13

Read verses 9-13 and record five observations about the disciples'
understanding of what would happen to Jesus.
What was Jesus' charge to the three?
Did they obey?
What puzzled the three disciples?
Why couldn't they understand what Jesus was telling them?
Who was to come before the Messiah? (Mal. 4:5)
Who did Jesus say Elijah was? (Matt. 17:13)
How did the one who was coming "restore all things"?
What was written about the Son of Man? (Num. 21:8-9 and John 3:14-
17)
What happened to John the Baptist? (Mark 6:27)
What do you think was the mood of the disciples as they returned to
the crowd? Were they puzzled, downcast, excited, or awed?

Today's challenge:
What do you think of the modern statement, "Of course, I believe
Jesus was the greatest prophet that ever lived"?
Is Jesus a prophet to you? More than a prophet?
Do you ever find yourself doubting God? When? Is that common?

Write today's challenge as a prayer:

Other prayers:

Questions for discussion or reflection:
How do you tell others about Jesus' majesty?
When have you wanted to tell about a spiritual mountaintop experi-
ence but didn't dare?
Why were you afraid to share your experience?
What experience shared by someone else really helped you?

LESSON 58

Rest peacefully in Jesus. Pray the prayer and review the Bible verse from Lesson 54.

Division 3: Passion, Mark 8:31—16:20
Unit 9: Crisis Week, Mark 8:31—9:29
Paragraph 5: The Great Failure, Mark 9:14-29

Read verses 14-29 and record five observations. What a contrast to the foregoing paragraph! Now watch the Servant. Imagine that this was your child. Try to feel the helplessness of the father, the scheming watchfulness of the teachers of the law, and the distress of the disciples.
How did the father describe the power of the spirit?
What power had the disciples been given? (Mark 6:7)
Jesus had now been with his disciples nearly three years. How did he express his pain and disappointment?
Describe Jesus' confrontation with the evil spirit. What did the spirit do? (verse 20)
Why did Jesus ask how long the spirit had afflicted the boy? What did the father call his faith?
What is the difference between unbelief and doubting faith?
What beautiful promise does Jesus give us all?
Notice the steps in the healing. Underline the verbs.
How did Jesus correctly identify the spirit?
What two commands did Jesus give the spirit?
What three things did the spirit do?
Notice how honestly the disciples accepted their failure. What did they lack?

Today's challenge:
If we are to take up the cross, what gift do we need?
Why are we and our church often weak?
Review the memory verse.
Have you ever recorded the time you spend in intercession in a day? In a week?

Write today's challenge as a prayer:

Other prayers:

Questions for discussion or reflection:
Discuss the difference between doubt and unbelief.
How can our churches help us face the reality of evil in the world today and still convey a strong sense of God's presence and power?

LESSON 59

Father, thank you for sending Jesus to earth. As we look at his long journey to Jerusalem, Jesus' courage and bravery overwhelms us. Was it because he looked fear squarely in the eye? Did he keep the cross constantly his passion? Father, help me to grow in my faith and take up the cross. Help me to see you as omnipotent, omnipresent, and omniscient! So many truths are concealed within Jesus' words as he journeyed to Jerusalem. Every time we study the journey, new truths can be revealed to us. Help us to see what Jesus thought was most important! Amen.

Bible verse: "For mortals it is impossible, but not for God; for God all things are possible." Mark 10:27

We have just finished the crisis week during which Christ began to teach his disciples that he was soon to die. He needed to teach them that if they wanted to be his disciples, they must take up their cross. This truth will be demonstrated as we study the longest journey in history—Jesus' journey to Jerusalem. Jesus had much to tell his disciples (and us) as he set his face toward the cross.

Division 3: Passion, Mark 8:31—16:20
Unit 10: Journey to Jerusalem, Mark 9:30—10:52
Paragraph 1: The Second Announcement, Mark 9:30-32

Study verses 30-32 and record five observations about Jesus' message.

Keep in mind the urgency of the moment and the teaching that was yet to be done as they walked through Galilee.

What three verbs did Jesus use to describe what was to happen?

What verb did Jesus mention twice?

Why did the word *betray* disturb the disciples?

Why didn't the disciples face the issue and ask Jesus what he meant? Do you think Jesus would have liked to discuss what he was saying with them?

Compare the verbs Jesus used in the first (8:31) and second (9:31) announcements of his upcoming death.

Today's challenge:

How are we, like the disciples, occupied with earthly thoughts when Jesus asks us to face the cross?

What issues are you and I sidestepping?

How could the disciples have communicated their fears and lack of understanding?

Write today's challenge as a prayer:

Other prayers:

Questions for discussion or reflection:

How is the communication in your home, with your spouse, children, and others?

Do you speak of the cross when trials come?

What fractured relationships exist in your neighborhood?

What emptiness in a person's life could you fill?

LESSON 60

Pray the prayer out loud and review the Bible verse from Lesson 59.

Division 3: Passion, Mark 8:31—16:20
Unit 10: Journey to Jerusalem, Mark 9:30—10:52
Paragraph 2: Who Is the Greatest? Mark 9:33-37

Study verses 33-37 and record five observations. What a pitiful contrast! Jesus had been talking about his humiliation and cross, and his disciples had been discussing their greatness.

Where were Jesus and his disciples now?

Notice Jesus' question and the disciples' silence.

Again Jesus used a visual image to illustrate his important point.

What are the characteristics of a child?

What do these verbs mean to you?

sat down

called

said

took

put

taking

What is true greatness in Jesus' kingdom?

What does the world think of Jesus' view of greatness?

What are the characteristics of a servant?

Today's challenge:

What is your response to greatness?

Do people today talk about heroes in sports or about those who study diligently?

How are the success stories of the world pressing in on us?

In whose name should we receive a child?

What are the two blessings when we do?

Write today's challenge as a prayer:

Other prayers:

Questions for discussion or reflection:

How can you practice verses 35-37 in your home?

What is your measuring stick—popularity, intelligence, beauty, style, financial success, or unselfish service?

LESSON 61

Offer quiet praise to God as you pray the prayer and review the Bible verse from Lesson 59.

Division 3: Passion, Mark 8:31—16:20
Unit 10: Journey to Jerusalem, Mark 9:30—10:52
Paragraph 3: For or Against?, Mark 9:38-41

Study verses 38-41 and record five observations about one's service to Christ. Review what happened in the previous paragraph.
Why do you think the incident described in verse 38 bothered John?
What powerful name did the man use in casting out the demon?
Wherein lies the power to cast out demons? (verse 39)
Why is Jesus' name so powerful? (Phil. 2:10, Eph. 3:20-21)
How did Jesus count success?
Just giving a cup of cold water may not seem to be important. Read Matt. 10:42. What is important and why?
What powerful word is mentioned three times in this paragraph? Also read Acts 4:12.

Today's challenge:
Have you ever tried to correct a person as John did?
Why is it difficult to use the name of Jesus in the presence of some people?
What was Jesus' response to John? To you and me?

Write today's challenge as a prayer:

Other prayers:

Questions for discussion or reflection:
Are you critical of others who cast out demons or do other good works in Jesus' name?
What people do you criticize because they are not a part of your denomination or group, or because they do not believe exactly as you do?

LESSON 62

Quietly praise God as you pray the prayer and review the Bible verse from Lesson 59.

Division 3: Passion, Mark 8:31—16:20
Unit 10: Journey to Jerusalem, Mark 9:30—10:52
Paragraph 4: Millstone, Mark 9:42-48
Paragraph 5: Salt, Mark 9:49-50

Study verses 42-50 and record five observations. Mark now began to reveal Jesus' marvelous lessons on the family.
With what family member did Jesus begin?
Notice the striking way Jesus cautioned his followers against the terrible act of misleading others. Here we see Jesus' wrath against hypocrisy, complacency, and domineering spirits. What angered Jesus the most?
What dreadful punishment did Jesus pronounce on those who destroy the faith of a child? (Check a Bible dictionary or encyclopedia to learn more about the millstone to which Jesus referred.)
What extreme examples did Jesus use to illustrate the enormity of the crime?
How did Jesus describe hell?
How many times did Jesus mention hell?
What do you think about hell?
Do you hear the reality of hell preached today?
What is the salt to which Jesus referred?
What does the salt do?
How do we have salt in ourselves and hence peace with one another?
How does self-discipline preserve us from self-corruption?
How do our lives produce thirst so that others will want to believe?

Today's challenge:
How would you feel about losing a foot, hand, or eye?
Does Jesus want us to mutilate our bodies?
What, then, does he want us to change?

Write today's challenge as a prayer:

Other prayers:

Questions for discussion or reflection:
Do those with broken hearts see the thirst and strength you get from the Word?
Are you hurting with them, approachable, or willing to become involved?
How can you be salt this week?

LESSON 63

Pray the prayer and review the Bible verse from Lesson 59.

Division 3: Passion, Mark 8:31—16:20
Unit 10: Journey to Jerusalem, Mark 9:30—10:52
Paragraph 6: Judea, Mark 10:1
Paragraph 7: Divorce, Mark 10:2-9

Study 10:1 and 10:2-1 and record five observations.
As this section begins, Jesus left what place for the last time?
Where did Jesus and his followers go?
What was Jesus still doing?
    Refer to a Bible dictionary to discover the Jews' two beliefs about divorce.
In Mark 10:2-9, what was the Pharisees' tricky question?
How did Jesus turn their point of attack?
Why did Jesus refer to Moses?
Why did Moses allow the Jews to divorce? (Deut. 24:1)
What was God's higher plan for marriage?

Today's challenge:
What is your beautiful picture of marriage?
What does it mean to become "one"?
What does "one" mean to you? Be definite.
How do we destroy marriage?
What is the challenge to marriage? (verse 9)
The greatest gift in a home is a father and mother who love God and each other!

Write today's challenge as a prayer:

Other prayers:

Questions for discussion or reflection:
How do we bring wholeness into a family?
Are there couples or families you should be praying for and helping?
How are you, individually and as a church, helping hurting families or single parents start a new beginning?
How can you help them conquer their fears?

LESSON 64

Pray the prayer and review the Bible verse from Lesson 59.

Division 3: Passion, Mark 8:31—16:20
Unit 10: Journey to Jerusalem, Mark 9:30—10:52
Paragraph 8: Marriage, Mark 10:10-12
Paragraph 9: Children, Mark 10:13-16

Study 10:10-16 and record five observations.
Why did Jesus give further teaching on divorce to his disciples?
According to verses 11-12, what constitutes adultery?
Notice that Jesus didn't have a double standard for divorce the way the Pharisees did. A husband and wife are equal.
According to Scripture, what are the two allowable reasons for divorce? (Matt. 5:32; 1 Cor. 7:15)
Who do you think suffers most when a divorce occurs?

Read Paragraph 9, Children, Mark 10:13-16
How beautiful! First Jesus talked about marriage, then children.
What gift did the people want Jesus to give the children?
Why did the people want Jesus to touch their children?
What does a look of love produce in a child?
Why did the disciples hinder the children?
Record two verbs that show Jesus' desire for the children.

Why must one be childlike to enter God's kingdom?
Record the three compassionate acts Jesus did for the children.

Today's challenge:
Today, honestly thank the Lord for each one in your family!
Have you touched each one of your family members today?
Have you said a word of kindness to each one? Have you hugged each one?

Write today's challenge as a prayer:

Other prayers:

Questions for discussion or reflection:
Children are to be raised in the "image of God," not my image or your image! Is that happening in your family?
How are the children in your life (your own, grandchildren, neighbors' children, ones you teach) able to share their visions, feelings, and true selves?
How do you accept children emotionally, physically, and spiritually?
Are they on the receiving edge of Jesus' love because you take time to listen? Have you told them they are special?
What hinders you from helping children know how much Christ loves them?

LESSON 65

Pray the prayer and review the Bible verse from Lesson 59.

Division 3: Passion, Mark 8:31—16:20
Unit 10: Journey to Jerusalem, Mark 9:30—10:52
Paragraph 10: Rich Young Man, Mark 10:17-22

Study verses 17-22 and record five observations about what it means to follow Jesus. Notice the central figure before Jesus.
What does Luke 10:25 reveal about this man?

What was wrong with the man's emphasis?

How did this man's ideas about God's kingdom compare with Jesus' explanation of the kingdom? (verse 15)

On what did this man base his faith?

How did Jesus feel about the man?

What did Jesus require from this man? List five actions in your notebook.

Compare the man's attitude at the beginning of the paragraph with his attitude at the end.

Today's challenge:

Notice Mark's beautiful sequence of events in these last paragraphs: the value of a child, the value of our own soul, marriage, children, and now possessions.

God has planned wonderful things for us if we will kick out the big "I" and allow the words of our memorized Bible verse to wash over us.

What do we need to get rid of?

What secret selfishness does Jesus need to lay bare in our hearts?

Write today's challenge as a prayer:

Other prayers:

Questions for discussion or reflection:

Name the barriers that keep you from following Jesus. What are your gods—pride, achievement, self-effort, sports, pleasure, money, popularity, self-pity, or low self-esteem?

Again, Jesus emphasizes that our trust in him demands all. Have you truly given him your mind, your heart, your attitude?

LESSON 66

In stillness before God, pray the prayer and review the Bible verse from Lesson 59.

Division 3: Passion, Mark 8:31—16:20
Unit 10: Journey to Jerusalem, Mark 9:30—10:52
Paragraph 11: Kingdom of God, Mark 10:23-27
Paragraph 12: Hundredfold, Mark 10:28-31

Study verses 23-31 and record five observations. Focus on how Jesus says one can enter the kingdom of God.
What topic did Jesus have to clarify?
Why were the disciples so amazed by what he said?
By what name did Jesus address the disciples?
What illustration did Jesus use to show the spiritual hazard of riches?
What puzzled the disciples?
What reward did Jesus promise to those who follow him?

Today's challenge:
In what ways are you trying to earn your way into the kingdom of God?
How have you experienced the truth expressed in verse 27?
When have you felt like Peter?
What does verse 31 mean to you?
Why is it hard for us to believe that we enter the kingdom only by God's grace, not by our achievement?

Write today's challenge as a prayer:

Other prayers:

Questions for discussion or reflection:
What is preventing you from giving your all to Jesus?
How are the values of this world reversed in the world to come?
What do you think of status, riches, or humility?
Has your family discussed your values? What values do you live by?

LESSON 67

Quietly praise God as you pray the prayer and review the Bible verse from Lesson 59.

Division 3: Passion, Mark 8:31—16:20
Unit 10: Journey to Jerusalem, Mark 9:30—10:52
Paragraph 13: The Third Announcement, Mark 10:32-34

Study verses 32-34 and record five observations about Jesus' announcement of his forthcoming death. Notice the procession. Imagine you are walking toward Jerusalem with Jesus.
Why were the disciples afraid of going to Jerusalem?
What scary word had Jesus mentioned in verse 30?
Do you feel the tension as Jesus broke the silence with his followers?
What is revealed in Jesus' third announcement of his death?
How does the word *Gentile* signify the kind of death Jesus will die?
Compare Jesus' three announcements of his death, noting how carefully Jesus reveals his impending suffering.
First—Mark 8:31
Second—Mark 9:31
Third—Mark 10:33-34
Do the other Gospel writers include the three predictions of Jesus' death? (Some Bibles include cross-references.)

Today's challenge:
What did you learn by comparing the three announcements of Jesus' death?
Is this study helping you see and understand Jesus' passion?

Write today's challenge as a prayer:

Other prayers:

Questions for discussion or reflection:
How does Jesus' third announcement impress you?
Has it become so commonplace that you pass it by, or can you share in Jesus' suffering as he enters his passion?

LESSON 68

Be still. Pray the prayer and review the Bible verse from Lesson 59.

Division 3: Passion, Mark 8:31—16:20
Unit 10: Journey to Jerusalem, Mark 9:30—10:52
Paragraph 14: James and John, Mark 10:35-40
Paragraph 15: Not to Be Served, but to Serve, Mark 10:41-45

Study verses 35-45 and record five observations about greatness in God's kingdom.
What kingdoms were James and John thinking about?
On what should they have focused their thoughts?
James and John belonged to the inner circle of three apostles (Mark 5:37; 9:2; 14:33). What did they ask of Jesus?
What kind of kingdom were James and John hanging on to?
What was beautiful about their request?
Notice Jesus' questions and the compassion with which he treated James and John. Why couldn't Jesus fulfill their request?
What is the "cup" and "baptism" Jesus spoke of here? (Rom. 6:3-4, Col. 2:12, Gal. 3:27)
Did James and John take the cup and baptism later in life? (Check a Bible dictionary if you don't know.)
Why did the other disciples become angry with James and John?
Notice how Jesus used this disagreement to teach more about greatness in God's kingdom.
Notice the three announcements 8:31; 9:31; and 10:32.
How does one rule in Jesus' kingdom? (Luke 14:11)

Today's challenge:
What is true greatness?
What makes verse 44 seem ridiculous to the world today?
Is the key verse becoming more meaningful to you? It reinforces the three divisions of the Gospel of Mark: He came (preparation), served (proclamation), and gave (passion).
Are you like the disciples, apt to be more impatient with the faults in others than the faults in yourself?

Do we seek to control our families and friends, or do we pray and relinquish them to the Lord?

Write today's challenge as a prayer:

Other prayers:

Questions for discussion or reflection:
How do you, like James and John, desire first place?
Are you trying to manage your workplace, your church, your family?
If you were to resign as chief manager and relinquish the reins, wouldn't you be more relaxed and a greater blessing?
How does Jesus' view of being a servant influence your daily life?

LESSON 69

Praise God as you repeat the prayer and Bible verse from Lesson 59.

Division 3: Passion, Mark 8:31—16:20
Unit 10: Journey to Jerusalem, Mark 9:30—10:52
Paragraph 16: Blind Bartimaeus, Mark 10:46-52

Study verses 46-52 and record five observations.
Where is Jericho? Check the map on page 240 to see how far it is from Jerusalem.
What three types of personalities do you find in the crowd?
Who do you think had witnessed to the blind man?
What astounding name does the blind beggar give Jesus?
What did that title mean?
Why was it important that the blind man had been told to keep still?
What did Jesus command?
Write down the three verbs that describe the man's actions.
Why did Jesus ask him what he wanted?
What verb did the blind man use in reply?

Today's challenge:
Why do you think Mark recorded this miracle?
What is Jesus ready to have proclaimed? By whom?

How are you proclaiming the Messiah?
How many spiritually blind people are living around you?
How many minutes a day do you spend in fervent prayer for them?

Write today's challenge as a prayer:

Other prayers:

Questions for discussion or reflection:
What type of person in the multitude are you most like?
Do you live close enough to Jesus to tell others that Jesus is as near to them as their own breath, that he will heal their brokenness?

LESSON 70

Jesus, come into the problems of my life and help me find peace. There are so many clashes in our homes and society and in the Body of Christ. Your Word says, "Let us work for the good of all, and especially for those of the family of faith" (Gal. 6:10). I cringe when I see myself joining hands with the priests, scribes, and elders in finding fault and judging.

Jesus, how I want your compassion, forgiveness, love, and joy. I ask for grace to receive these gifts, Father. I know the best way is through praise, so I ask for the blessing of praise today through every trial. Help me to meet the mundane confusion of life in forgiveness of myself and others.

I await your blessings! Thank you, Jesus! Amen.

Bible verse: "Whenever you stand praying, forgive, if you have anything against anyone; so that your Father in heaven may also forgive you your trespasses." Mark 11:25

Division 3: Passion, Mark 8:31—16:20
Unit 11: Clashes in the Temple, Mark 11:1—12:44
Paragraph 1: Triumphant Entry, Mark 11:1-10

Study 11:1-10 and record five observations. Keep in mind that the

Jews had looked for the Messiah for thousands of years. At the time Jesus rode into Jerusalem, Jews had traveled to Jerusalem from all over the Roman world for a week-long, exciting celebration to commemorate the Passover (Exodus 12).

Jesus had allowed himself to be declared the Messiah. Now, perfectly timed, he allowed himself to be declared the promised King of Israel. What a majestic, calm, humble, powerful, and brilliant King we have! Use your imagination and enjoy the scene as you see the King of Israel marching on.

Locate Jerusalem, Bethphage, and Bethany on the map on page 240. What were Jesus' specific directions to his two disciples? Focus on the verbs he used.

Why do you think they got the colt so easily?

Notice how the people honored Jesus.

How did the people fulfill the prophecy from five hundred years before Christ? (Zech. 9:9)

How did Jesus' entrance fit his character?

How did kings usually ride into a city?

Why did the people spread clothes and leafy branches on the road?

Why were the people so excited? (John 12:9-19)

Where had the crowd heard Jesus called the "Son of David" before? (Mark 10:47-48)

How did the people's actions fulfill the prophecies of old? (Ps. 24:7-10; Zech. 9:9)

What did the crowd expect from Jesus? (John 6:15)

What do you think the disciples expected from Jesus?

Today's challenge:
What does the word *blessed* mean to you?

Praise Jesus by reading the song of praise many times (Mark 11:9-10).

Do you listen and obey the exact directions Jesus gives to you?

How is Jesus riding into your daily life?

Are you excited about him? If not, why not?

Write today's challenge as a prayer:

Other prayers:

Questions for discussion or reflection:
What do you love most about Jesus' triumphant entry?

How do you praise Jesus one day, shun him the next day, are too busy the next day, or misunderstand him the next day?

How can you handle this inconsistency better?
How does this scene impress on you that emotion cannot be a substitute for faith?

LESSON 71

Pray the prayer and review the Bible verse from Lesson 70.

Division 3: Passion, Mark 8:31—16:20
Unit 11: Clashes in the Temple, Mark 11:1—12:44
Paragraph 2: Temple Inspection, Mark 11:11
Paragraph 3: Jesus curses a Fig Tree, Mark 11:12-14

Study and record five observations. Use a Bible encyclopedia as a reference and try to visualize Herod's temple.
On what day of the week did Jesus inspect the temple?
What verbs describe Jesus?
Where did he go next?
The next day Jesus used a fig tree to make an important point. Why was Jesus hungry?
Refer to a Bible dictionary or encyclopedia to learn what you can about fig trees.
Why did Jesus expect fruit from the fig tree?
What picture of Israel as a nation does this give us?
What fruit did Israel produce?

Today's challenge:
How do we produce "nothing but leaves"?
What insight is the Holy Spirit giving you?

Write today's challenge as a prayer:

Other prayers:

Questions for discussion or reflection:
How do we hide your fruitlessness with leaves in your home? In your community or business? In your church?

What is the fruit of the Spirit? (Gal. 5:22-23)
What is the opposite of bearing fruit? (Gal. 5:19-21)

LESSON 72

Pray the prayer and review the Bible verse from Lesson 70. Do you know you are forgiven?

Division 3: Passion, Mark 8:31—16:20
Unit 11: Clashes in the Temple, Mark 11:1—12:44
Paragraph 4: Cleansing of the Temple, Mark 11:15-19

Read verses 15-19 and record five observations about Jesus' actions and others' reactions.
   This was Monday of Jesus' final week in Jerusalem. What Jesus thought about doing Sunday night, he did on Monday.
Record five action verbs that describe what Jesus did in the temple.
What should the temple be? For whom?
Why was Jesus angry about the buying and selling that took place in the temple? (Isa. 56:6-8)
What is a den of robbers? (Jer. 7:11)
Was it wrong for Jesus to become angry? (Mal. 3:3)
What commandment did the priests and scribes plan to break?
How does this paragraph relate to the previous paragraph we studied? (verses 12-14)
Where did Jesus and his disciples go at night? Why?

Today's challenge:
When did you last become angry about some injustice and do something about it?
Is God calling you to become involved in some issues?

Write today's challenge as a prayer:

Other prayers:

Questions for discussion or reflection:
How could your church become a vibrant house of evangelism and prayer?
Where would Jesus start cleaning in your church?

LESSON 73

Pray the prayer and review the Bible verse from Lesson 70. Rest in forgiveness!

Division 3: Passion, Mark 8:31—16:20
Unit 11: Clashes in the Temple, Mark 11:1—12:44
Paragraph 5: Fig Tree Withered, Mark 11:20-24
Paragraph 6: Forgive, Mark 11:25-26

Study verses 20-26 and record five observations. (In some Bibles, verse 26 will appear in footnote.) Jesus and his disciples had again slept outside the city, and returning at night, they did not see the withered fig tree.
What day was this?
What is implied in Peter's statement?
The disciples had seen Jesus cleanse the temple and now they saw the withered fig tree. How are these events related to the spiritual state of the Jewish nation?
Jesus took the example of his curse and from it produced a greater lesson. What was this lesson?
To what kind of "mountains" did Jesus refer?
What power did he say the disciples would have?
What steps for prayer do you find in paragraph 6?
What is the most important thing to do when praying?

Today's challenge:
What prevents God from answering our prayers?
Do you really pray for forgiveness when you pray the Lord's Prayer?
When one member of the body of Christ hurts, we all hurt! Where is Jesus calling you to get involved?

Write today's challenge as a prayer:

Other prayers:

Questions for discussion or reflection:
What seems like a mountain in your life?
On what conditions does God answer prayer?
Can you believe "that what he says will come to pass"?
Have you learned to be silent so you can hear God's answers?

LESSON 74

Pray the prayer and review the Bible verse from Lesson 70. Thank God for the joy of forgiveness!

Division 3: Passion, Mark 8:31—16:20
Unit 11: Clashes in the Temple, Mark 11:1—12:44
Paragraph 7: First Clash, Mark 11:27-33

Study verses 27-33 and record five observations. Focus on the way Jesus handled those who challenged him.
This was Tuesday morning of the last week. What was Jesus doing?
Who was ready to challenge him?
Why did they feel they had a right to challenge him?
What was the first clash?
To what did "these things" refer?
What were they trying to force Jesus to confess?
What clever counter dilemma did Jesus put them in?
Notice how Jesus countered their attack with a clever question. Whom did Jesus substitute for himself in the question?

Why was the real question not one of authority, but of obedience? Notice the argument that ensued among his accusers and their pitiful, disgraceful surrender. Their trickery backfired!
How did they dodge the issue?
How did Jesus' answer make them appear before the people?
Review the first clash. Who was involved?
What was the question?
What was Jesus' answer?
What effect did the clash have?

Today's challenge:
How much do you use Jesus' authority in your prayers? In praying for yourself? In praying for others? In your daily life?

Write today's challenge as a prayer:

Other prayers:

Questions for discussion or reflection:
Do you really believe Jesus has all authority in heaven and on earth? How do you see his authority? Why doesn't everyone recognize it? How can you use his authority in your prayers?

LESSON 75

Pray the prayer and review the Bible verse from Lesson 70.

Division 3: Passion, Mark 8:31—16:20
Unit 11: Clashes in the Temple, Mark 11:1—12:44
Paragraph 8: Vineyard, Mark 12:1-11

Study verses 1-11 and record five observations about Jesus' continuing response to the chief priests, scribes, and elders.
Why did Jesus speak in parables?
Notice how cleverly Jesus exposed the Sanhedrin's hypocrisy and sneaky ways by telling a story!

What did the vineyard the man had prepared represent?
Whom did the tenants represent? The servants?

This parable does not center our attention on the vineyard or on the amount of fruit produced, but on the action of the tenants.
What did they do to the servants the owner sent?
First servant:
Second servant:
Third servant and others:
Son:

What was Jesus saying about his enemies?
Notice how God's love and patience exceeded all bounds by sending his Son.
What did this parable reveal the owner would do?
How did Jesus predict and expose his accusers' plans through this parable?
Jesus must have told this parable dramatically. How did the people respond? (Luke 20:16b)
Here Jesus quoted from the messianic psalm, Ps. 118:22-23. Who is the stone?
How does this parable answer Jesus' right of authority? (verses 27-33)

Today's challenge:
The story of the vineyard shows God's relationship with the religious leaders of the day.
What do you think of it?
How do you welcome Jesus in your church meetings?

Write today's challenge as a prayer:

Other prayers:

Questions for discussion or reflection:
If you were going on a trip, to whom would you entrust your vineyard or business? Why?
If a stranger came to your church, would Jesus have the chance to welcome him or her through you?
How do you make Jesus welcome in your home?

LESSON 76

Pray the prayer and review the Bible verse from Lesson 70.

Division 3: Passion, Mark 8:31—16:20
Unit 11: Clashes in the Temple, Mark 11:1—12:44
Paragraph 9: Fear of the Crowd, Mark 12:12
Paragraph 10: Second Clash, Mark 12:13-17

Study 12:12 and 12:13-17 and record five observations about those who wanted to trap Jesus.
Why were many people in Jerusalem?
Why was it dangerous to try to arrest Jesus?
Had Jesus' enemies understood the meaning of the parable?
Notice who the Sanhedrin chose as partners in their efforts to discredit Jesus (Mark 12:13). Watch their hypocrisy and flattery.
What words of Jesus exposed them?
What was the significance of the coin Jesus asked for?
How did Jesus handle the clash?
Review the second clash. Who was involved?
What was the question?
What was Jesus' answer?
What effect did his reply have?

Today's challenge:
Take a look at a U.S. dime, nickel, penny, or quarter. What is the inscription? Do you?
How often do you thank God for liberty? For living in a nation where he can be worshiped?
How active are you in fighting the evils in our nation?
Are you leaving the job to someone else?

Write today's challenge as a prayer:

Other prayers:

Questions for discussion or reflection:
How deeply should you be involved in political issues?
Can you bear God's image in politics?
Whom do you know who does?
How do you keep informed about the principles taught in our schools?

LESSON 77

Be still before God and pray the prayer and review the Bible verse from Lesson 70.

Division 3: Passion, Mark 8:31—16:20
Unit 11: Clashes in the Temple, Mark 11:1—12:44
Paragraph 11: Third Clash, Mark 12:18-23
Paragraph 12: God of the Living, Mark 12:24-27

Study 12:18-27 and record five observations. Refer to a Bible dictionary to find out what the Sadducees believed.
What was their real question?
How did Jesus puncture the Sadducees' argument? List his two main points in your notebook.
How did Jesus explain their blindness?
Will we be angels in heaven?
Notice Jesus' power-packed statement about who God is!
What does "living" mean to you?
Compare Mark 12:27 (notice the present tense of the verb) with 1 Cor. 15:12-28.
Feel the bite of Jesus' last statement, "You are quite wrong!"
How do you think the Sadducees responded to this statement?
Review the third clash. Who was involved?
What was the question?
What was Jesus' answer?

What effect did it have?

Today's challenge:
How powerful is verse 27 to you?
Does each day offer hope of resurrection?
Do you know Scripture so you can know death, life, and the power of the resurrection?

Write today's challenge as a prayer:

Other prayers:

Questions for discussion or reflection:
Are you afraid of death?
Are you intimidated to talk about death?
Why should a Christian be excited about heaven?

LESSON 78

Pray the prayer and review the Bible verse from Lesson 70. Are you learning to forgive?

Division 3: Passion, Mark 8:31—16:20
Unit 11: Clashes in the Temple, Mark 11:1—12:44
Paragraph 13: Fourth Clash, Mark 12:28-34

Study verses 28-34 and record five observations about obedience to God. Over the years 613 laws and requirements had been added to the Ten Commandments. With all these laws, deciding which were the most important was a problem.
Who asked the question now? (Matt. 22:35)
How was this clash different from the clashes in 11:28; 12:14; and 12:23?
How did Jesus' answer relate to Deut. 6:5?
What commandment does Deut. 6:5 encompass?
What commandment does Lev. 19:18 encompass?

Mark 12:29-30 was to be recited daily by every adult Jewish male.
How did the scribe answer?
How important are burnt offerings and sacrifices? (1 Corinthians 13, Mic. 6:6-8)

Again, Jesus was victor. Think of how Jesus clashed with the scribes and Pharisees, minimizing their 613 laws.
What do you think of Jesus' challenge to the scribe?
What should have been the scribe's next step?
What was the result of this clash on the crowd?
Review the fourth clash. Who was involved?
What was the question?
What was the answer?
What effect did it have?

Today's challenge:
How much do you love the Lord?
When last did you tell him you loved him?
Don't we as individuals like to hear we are loved?
Write a paragraph of thanksgiving and love to Jesus!

Write today's challenge as a prayer:

Other prayers:

Questions for discussion or reflection:
Whom do you love the most—God, neighbor, or self?
How can you begin to love God more? To love yourself? To love your neighbor?

LESSON 79

In stillness before God, pray the prayer and review the Bible verse from Lesson 70.

Division 3: Passion, Mark 8:31—16:20
Unit 11: Clashes in the Temple, Mark 11:1—12:44
Paragraph 14: Son of David, Mark 12:35-37

Paragraph 15: Long Robes and Prayers, Mark 12:38-40

Study verses 35-40 and record five observations.
What was Jesus doing in the temple?
What should that show us? (Deut. 6:7)
Now Jesus asked the people the same question that he had asked the disciples in Mark 8:29. What was the question?
Why was it important?

Read Psalm 110, which is the psalm of David that Jesus quoted here.
Identify the following:
Who is the Lord?
My Lord?
My right hand?
I?
Your?
What, then, did David call Jesus?

Notice who was willing to learn from Jesus.
The Pharisees knew the Scriptures. How was Jesus trying to win even his enemies?
What was Jesus' supreme claim?
Why did Jesus condemn the scribes in public (Mark 12:38-40)?
Restate his charge in modern terms.
What reward would they receive?

Today's challenge:
Why is it wrong to use our spirituality to gain praise or recognition?
Do we extol the so-called famous and ignore the faithful?
List some of the faithful you admire!

Write today's challenge as a prayer:

Other prayers:

Questions for discussion or reflection:
How does love rule in your home relationships, among your neighbors, and in your church?
What do we do when pride and selfishness seem to take over?

LESSON 80

Pray the prayer and review the Bible verse from Lesson 70.

Division 3: Passion, Mark 8:31—16:20
Unit 11: Clashes in the Temple, Mark 11:1—12:44
Paragraph 16: The Widow's Coins, Mark 12:41-44

Study verses 41-44 and record five observations. Take a look at Jesus in this paragraph. After that difficult discourse, he calmly watched the scene about him.
What day was this and where was Jesus?
Why was the widow's gift so significant?
What were Jesus' first words after the widow gave her gift?
By giving her last cent, what did the widow really do?

Today's challenge:
Compare this woman with the scribes described in the preceding paragraph.
Do you tithe? Why or why not?
Who are you most like—the scribes or the woman?

Write today's challenge as a prayer:

Other prayers:

Questions for discussion or reflection:
What is your motive in giving?
Does the thought of tithing trigger a guilt complex?
How do we give our all—not only in terms of money, but also in terms of helping those who are imprisoned in fears, caught in bondages of self-destruction, or suffering from disease or sin?

LESSON 81

Jesus, it's so exciting to know you are coming again! Christians do disagree about when you are coming, but help me to live in the daily joy of knowing that you are coming and that you are preparing a place for me. Sometimes your coming fills me with fear. But is that okay, Jesus, when I've never experienced it before, and you are so holy?

Whether I die through illness, or accident, or old age, or meet you in the skies, may I live in your glorious victory over death. Imprint on my heart and mind—watch, watch, watch! Amen!

Bible verse: "Beware that no one leads you astray." Mark 13:5

Division 3: Passion, Mark 8:31—16:20
Unit 12: Future Events, Mark 13:1-37
Paragraph 1: Not One Stone, Mark 13:1-2
Paragraph 2: Signs in the World, Mark 13:3-8

Study verses 1-8 and record five observations.

In order to understand Unit 12, we must consider two events: first, the destruction of the temple in A.D. 70 by the armies of Rome, which was doomsday for the Jewish nation; second, Christ's second coming, which spells doomsday for the world. Also, keep in mind that the figurative language in this chapter often leads to honest differences of opinion as to the interpretation.

This was still Tuesday, at the end of the day. Jesus was leaving the temple for the last time to go to Bethany.

What did the disciples marvel at as they left the temple?

How complete did Jesus say the destruction of the temple would be?

What did the temple mean to the disciples?

Why did Jesus turn the disciples' observation into a look at the end times?

Look at verse 3. Where were Jesus and his disciples now?

After hearing Jesus' drastic prediction, what two things did the disciples want to know?

Jesus preceded his explanation with a warning. What was it?
Jesus listed four signs that must take place before the temple is destroyed. What were those signs? List them in your notebook.

Today's challenge:
Are you praying and looking for Jesus' coming?
Does Jesus' coming fill you with fear, awe, or joy?
With whom have you shared your feelings?
Is it common to live in fear of something we haven't experienced before?

Write today's challenge as a prayer:

Other prayers:

Questions for discussion or reflection:
What do you think about people who claim special knowledge of the day Jesus is coming?
How prepared are you for his coming? Are you afraid to face it?

LESSON 82

Pray the prayer and review the Bible verse from Lesson 81.

Division 3: Passion, Mark 8:31—16:20
Unit 12: Future Events, Mark 13:1-37
Paragraph 3: Signs in the Local Community, Mark 13:9-13

Study verses 9-13 and record five observations about the hardship and hope of which the disciples will be a part. This was Tuesday evening before the awful Friday of the crucifixion.
What was Jesus speaking about? (verse 10)
Notice Jesus' concern for the disciples, although he never withheld the coming trials or difficulties of their task. For what three reasons were the disciples to beware? Write them in your notebook.
Did this come true? (See Acts 22:19; 26:11; 2 Cor. 11:24-25.)

Why will the Holy Spirit speak for those who follow Christ?
Why is the persecution mentioned in verse 12 so difficult?
Why will Christ's followers be hated?
What glorious promise is given to those who endure?
What will be the disciples' supreme task?

Today's challenge:
Why does persecution bother us? What difficulties and hardships do we face as followers of Christ?

Write today's challenge as a prayer:

Other prayers:

Questions for discussion or reflection:
Imagine yourself as one of the disciples. How do you think they responded to what Jesus told them?
What would happen to his disciples and the church?
How are you facing all the messages on TV and in print that are contradictory to the Christian faith?

LESSON 83

Be still before God and pray the prayer and review the Bible verse from Lesson 81.

Division 3: Passion, Mark 8:31—16:20
Unit 12: Future Events, Mark 13:1-37
Paragraph 4: Signs in the Church, Mark 13:14-23

Study 13:14-23 and record five observations. In the first three paragraphs of this unit, Jesus had spoken comprehensively covering the whole time from his own day to the end of the world. He next turned to the destruction of Jerusalem in particular, an event of great importance for the twelve disciples and their work.
This prophecy is also of vital importance for future ages because it stands as a "type," a picture, of the end of the world.

What is the "desolating sacrilege" about which Jesus warned his disciples? (Matt. 24:15 and Dan. 11:31)

When should the people of Judea flee?

Notice the four descriptions of haste. Write them in your notebook.

Notice Jesus' compassion. How his heart melted at the thought of these trials for his elect (verses 17-18). The fanatical Jewish rebellion that led to lasted about five years (verse 20). Jesus did not want the Jews to annihilate themselves, and so what did he promise to do?

Who are the "elect"?

What is the profound warning in verse 21?

Today's challenge:

Are you afraid to talk about these times? Why or why not?

How much time do you spend praying for your unsaved relatives and friends?

Write today's challenge as a prayer:

Other prayers:

Questions for discussion or reflection:

How are Christians led astray or deceived?

Is the Bible your standard for your actions? Common sense? Others' arguments?

How much do you live in the Word? Time yourself for a week!

LESSON 84

Pray the prayer and review the Bible verse from Lesson 81.

Division 3: Passion, Mark 8:31—16:20
Unit 12: Future Events, Mark 13:1-37
Paragraph 5: Signs in the Sky, Mark 13:24-27
Paragraph 6: Signs in the Fig Tree, Mark 13:28-31

Study 13:24-31 and record five observations about "those days." To what does "in those days" refer?
What four signs in the sky did Jesus mention? List them in your notebook.
How will Jesus come? (Read 1 Thess. 4:16 too.)
How will Jesus gather his elect?
Who are the angels?

Read paragraph 6, The Fig Tree, again.
Why did Jesus use the fig tree as his example?
Turn again to Mark 11:12-14. How is the fig tree compared to the end of time?
What does a generation mean?
Why won't God's Word ever pass away?
How was this a comfort, or a discomfort, to the disciples?

Today's challenge:
Are you afraid of Jesus' coming, or are you living in expectancy?
Would you like Jesus to return tomorrow? Why or why not?
How powerful is the Word that goes forth from your mouth? (Isa. 55:10-11)
Do you believe this?

Write today's challenge as a prayer:

Other prayers:

Questions for discussion or reflection:
What lesson do you learn from the "fig tree" as you see "these things" taking place?
Do you believe Christ is coming soon?
Do you pray, "Come, Lord Jesus"?

LESSON 85

Pray the prayer and review the Bible verse from Lesson 81.

Division 3: Passion, Mark 8:31—16:20
Unit 12: Future Events, Mark 13:1-37
Paragraph 7: Keep Awake, Mark 13:32-37

Study 13:32-37 and record five observations about Jesus' warnings to keep alert.
Who alone knows "the day or hour"?
Why doesn't Jesus know?
What is Jesus' warning to us?
How many times are "keep alert" or "keep awake" used in this paragraph (some versions say "watch")?
Whom does the man going on a journey represent?
Why did Jesus use the figurative language of a doorkeeper?
How would one be sleeping?
How can we help each other "watch"?
What word is repeated in verses 5, 9, and 33? What word with a similar meaning is repeated in verses 23, 33, and 37?

Today's challenge:
In what ways are you excited about Christ's second coming? How are you keeping alert? In what ways are you afraid?

Write today's challenge as a prayer:

Other prayers:

Questions for discussion or reflection:
How are you living out verses 34 and 37?
Do you study and discuss Christ's second coming in your church? Your family?
If we are to watch, what are we to be doing?

LESSON 86

Father, in this unit I will deal with the gruesomeness of Jesus' arrest and trial. It has become such common knowledge to me that I no longer cringe when I read that he gave his life as a ransom for all. Imprint on my mind what the word ransom *encompasses. But I do stand in awe as I watch Jesus' love abundantly poured out on everyone, even overflowing to those who mistreat him and refuse to believe. Today, give me the gift of your willingness to love the unlovely. Amen.*

Bible verse: "He said, 'Abba, Father, for you all things are possible; remove this cup from me; yet, not what I want, but what you want.' " Mark 14:36

Division 3: Passion, Mark 8:31—16:20
Unit 13: The Arrest and Trial, Mark 14:1—15:15
Paragraph 1: Plot to Kill, Mark 14:1-2
Paragraph 2: The Anointing, Mark 14:3-9

Study 14:1-9 and record five observations. Jesus now had one passion— to die. Keep the name of this unit in mind, "The Arrest and Trial."
What day was it?
Establish the time of year and feast clearly in your mind (Luke 22:7, Exod. 12:1-36).
How did Jesus frustrate the plans of the Sanhedrin?
What did their plans reveal about the spiritual and moral standards of the Jewish nation?
Why were so many people in Jerusalem at this time?

Read Paragraph 2, Mark 14:3-9, again. For some reason, Mark placed this beautiful act of anointing in direct contrast to the evil act of Jesus' enemies.
In whose home were Jesus and the disciples? Why?
Who was the woman who anointed Jesus in love? (John 12:1-8)
What were the hidden motives of those who criticized this woman?
Why was this gift of ointment so extravagant?

119

What would you do with such a costly gift?

Why was Mary so intent on her act of love? Do you think Mary sensed that Jesus would soon die?

How did Jesus justify Mary's action?

Today's challenge:

Have you done what you could to honor Jesus?

Is criticism festering in your mind?

How will criticism destroy you if you don't give it to Jesus?

What is held before our eyes in newspapers and TV today—the famous or the faithful?

Are we mentally influenced by what we admire?

Write today's challenge as a prayer:

Other prayers:

Questions for discussion or reflection:

Do our Sunday offerings dampen our conscience so that we don't get involved with the poor?

What sacrificial gift would you like to give Jesus, even if it might seem foolish to others?

LESSON 87

Pray the prayer and review the Bible verse from Lesson 86.

Division 3: Passion, Mark 8:31—16:20
Unit 13: The Arrest and Trial, Mark 14:1—15:15
Paragraph 3: Judas's Plot, Mark 14:10-11
Paragraph 4: The Passover, Mark 14:12-16

Study 14:10-16 and record five observations.

How low had Judas stooped?

What was Judas's motive in betraying Jesus?

How low had the delighted chief priests stooped?

For how much did Judas betray Jesus? (Matt. 26:15)
How do you think Judas felt about his act?
Now look at Paragraph 4, Mark 14:12-16, again. What day was this?
What do you think Jesus did on Wednesday, the day before Passover?
Refer to a Bible encyclopedia and find out what was involved in preparing the Passover feast.
Why were the disciples concerned about preparations for the Passover feast? (Exodus 12)
What risk did Jesus face at Passover?
Do you have any idea who the man carrying a jar of water was, or who the owner of the house was?

Today's challenge:
Would you compare the Passover feast to our Easter or to our Christmas?
How well do I follow Jesus' direction?

Write today's challenge as a prayer:

Other prayers:

Questions for discussion or reflection:
It's easy to point fingers at Judas, but how well do you handle your commitment to Christ?
In trying circumstances, when have you denied Jesus, betrayed him, or rejected his authority?

LESSON 88

Pray the prayer and review the Bible verse from Lesson 86.

Division 3: Passion, Mark 8:31—16:20
Unit 13: The Arrest and Trial, Mark 14:1—15:15
Paragraph 5: Is It I? Mark 14:17-21
Paragraph 6: The Lord's Supper, Mark 14:22-25

Study verses 17-25 and record five observations about this unique

Passover feast. Notice the divine foreknowledge of the courageous Servant.

What evening is being described?

Who were the invited guests?

What sad, shocking news must Jesus relate?

What word describes the disciples?

Notice the gentle way Jesus exposed Judas. What warning did Jesus give him?

In what way was the Son of Man still in control?

Read Paragraph 6, Mark 14:22-25, again. Record Jesus' ten words of action in your notebook.

How much did the disciples understand as Jesus spoke of his body and blood?

Refer to a Bible encyclopedia to learn what a covenant is. What happened to the old covenant?

Compare verse 25 with Rev. 19:9. How did this meal give the disciples and us insight on what Jesus was about to do on the cross?

Today's challenge:

Do you ever fear that you might betray Jesus?

What strength does this holy sacrament give us?

Do we thank Jesus for this immeasurable gift?

Write today's challenge as a prayer:

Other prayers:

Questions for discussion or reflection:

What does the Lord's Supper mean in your life?

Do you partake of Communion so often that it has become commonplace?

Is Communion a means of receiving forgiveness, joy, strength?

Why is the Lord's Supper important for the body of Christ?

LESSON 89

Pray the prayer and review the Bible verse from Lesson 86.

Division 3: Passion, Mark 8:31—16:20
Unit 13: The Arrest and Trial, Mark 14:1—15:15
Paragraph 7: Prediction, Mark 14:26-31
Paragraph 8: Gethsemane, Mark 14:32-42

Study 14:26-42 and record five observations. Imagine, Jesus sang a hymn at this time, probably a psalm!
Where were Jesus and the disciples going?
What tragedy did Jesus say would befall the disciples?
To what did Jesus compare this tragedy?
What two hopeful promises did Jesus give the disciples?
What cocky statement did Peter make? How did he feel about it later?
Why did Jesus warn the disciples, Peter particularly, about their coming denial of him?
What was Peter's motivation? Did he feel superior to the other disciples, or was he expressing love for Jesus?
What did Peter mention, for the first time, he was willing to do?
Can you imagine the other disciples echoing Peter's words?
Try to imagine how the disciples must have pondered these words after Jesus had been crucified and buried.

Read Paragraph 8, Mark 14:32-42, once more. Mark tried to reveal Jesus' intense suffering to us! Today, imagine yourself as one of Jesus' disciples. Meditate on Jesus' stunning words at the Passover meal as you leave the upper room and walk toward the Mount of Olives, cross the Brook of Kidron, and enter the Garden of Gethsemane. Feel the cool night air, the darkness of night, the breeze rustling the olive trees.

Notice Jesus' face and how he presses on. As he goes to pray, he is "greatly distressed and agitated." Feel his utter aloneness as he is forsaken by his disciples. Is he separated from his Father too?

Hear Jesus' soul cry, "Abba, Father . . . remove this cup." How terrible it was to take the cup, to bear all the sins of the whole world.

See Jesus again and again prostrate in prayer, receiving no human sympathy. As his soul's agony becomes intolerable, he continues to pray, lying prostrate on the ground. The cup is not removed, but the Father sends grace. Death loses its sting, and the grave has given up its power. He rises to victory!

Today's challenge:
This is what Jesus suffered for me! He bore my sins and my extended family's sins; the sins of my church, community, state, and country; and the sins of the seven continents, islands, the world. Never will I fathom the depth of his love, but in heaven I will praise him forever!

Write today's challenge as a prayer:

Other prayers:

Questions for discussion or reflection:
Will Jesus' beautiful "Yet, not what I want, but what you want" change your will today?
What is your Gethsemane? Are you too busy, your eyes too heavy?

LESSON 90

Be still before God and pray the prayer and review the Bible verse from Lesson 86.

Division 3: Passion, Mark 8:31—16:20
Unit 13: The Arrest and Trial, Mark 14:1—15:15
Paragraph 9: Betrayal, Mark 14:43-50
Paragraph 10: Young Man, Mark 14:51-52
Paragraph 11: Trial before the High Priest, Mark 14:53-65

Study verses 43-65 and record five observations.
Where did Jesus' arrest take place?
Who met Jesus?

Notice who had sent the crowd, and the irony of the swords and the betrayer's despicable acts. Turn to John 18:4-11 and take in that powerful image of Jesus. See how he perfectly mastered the situation. All that occurred did so only with his consent.

How did Jesus reveal the crowd's cowardly act?

Compare verse 50 with verses 27 and 31.

Read Paragraph 10, Mark 14:51-52, again. Who do you think this young man was?

Read Paragraph 11, Mark 14:53-65, again. Who was the high priest? (Matt. 26:57)

Here we have the Sanhedrin. Review Lesson 54 to recall what this group was.

Peter apparently recovered enough to follow Jesus. What does this tell you about Peter?

How did Peter get into the courtyard? (John 18:16)

Why couldn't the council put Jesus to death?

What temple had Jesus spoken of? (John 2:21)

The trial was not going too well. Notice the high priest's predicament.

How did he try to incriminate Jesus?

Why did Jesus remain silent? (Luke 22:67)

What was the high priest's all-important question?

What was Jesus' powerful answer?

Why did the high priest tear his clothes?

What six verbs describe the council's treatment of Jesus? Write them in your notebook.

Today's challenge:

Meditate on the utter fear of the disciples. Have you ever run away from something?

Write today's challenge as a prayer:

Other prayers:

Questions for discussion or reflection:

How do you face a crisis?

When have you been tempted to make hasty judgments like the Sanhedrin made?

What help do you need to stand as Jesus did?

LESSON 91

Pray the prayer and review the Bible verse from Lesson 86.

Division 3: Passion, Mark 8:31—16:20
Unit 13: The Arrest and Trial, Mark 14:1—15:15
Paragraph 12: The Denial, Mark 14:66-72
Paragraph 13: Trial before Pilate, Mark 15:1-5

Study 14:66—15:5 and record five observations. Keep in mind that we believe Peter told these stories to Mark.
Where was Peter? (Mark 14:54)
How do you think Peter felt?
Record the servant girl and bystanders' three observations in your notebook.
Record Peter's answers.
How are the three denials alike?
How did Peter's denial increase Jesus' pain?
What brought Peter to his senses? (Mark 14:30, John 18:27)
Look again at Paragraph 13, Mark 15:1-5. What does "as soon as it was morning" mean?
Who was the whole council? Check a Bible encyclopedia if you don't know.
Recall the word *betrayed* (Mark 9:31). How is that word being fulfilled here?
Who was Pilate?
Why do you think Pilate asked Jesus the first question?
Did Jesus say he was King of the Jews?
What were the accusations against Jesus?
What was Pilate's sin?

Today's challenge:
Name an incident where you could identify with Peter.
What "rooster" aroused you?
When have sidestepped an issue?
When have you been disappointed in yourself? What did you do about it?

Write today's challenge as a prayer:

Other prayers:

Questions for discussion or reflection:
It's easy to look with contempt on the Jewish leaders, but when, like the disciples, have you inflicted shame on Jesus and denied him?

LESSON 92

Pray the prayer and review the Bible verse from Lesson 86.

Division 3: Passion, Mark 8:31—16:20
Unit 13: The Arrest and Trial, Mark 14:1—15:15
Paragraph 14: Barabbas, Mark 15:6-15

Study 15:6-15 and record five observations.
What feast was this? (John 18:39)
Was releasing a prisoner Pilate's idea?
What do we know about Barabbas?
What do you think the Sanhedrin thought of the name Pilate gave Jesus (twice)?
Why was Pilate anxious to release Jesus? (Mark 15:10, Matt. 27:19, 23)
Why had the crowd changed so since Palm Sunday?
Why is the idea of crucifixion so shocking?
Why was the verdict so terrible, physically and emotionally? Why did Pilate give in to the crowd? (John 19:11-12) (See also Matt. 27:24-25.)
How was Scripture being fulfilled through these events? (Matt. 26:2, John 11:50, Mark 10:45)

Today's challenge:
When have your actions or words failed to witness for Jesus? Record one or more incidents. How did you feel? What did you do about it?

Write today's challenge as a prayer:

Other prayers:

Questions for discussion or reflection:
How does this treatment of Jesus make you feel?
Would you have dared take his side?
How have your actions mocked the name of Jesus?

LESSON 93

I know that my Redeemer lives!
What comfort this sweet sentence gives!
He lives, he lives, who once was dead;
He lives, my everliving head.

Thank you, Jesus, for the freedom, the joy in you! What a new be-
ginning your life means every hour, every day, every year. Help me
grasp the freedom of telling the gospel to every creature. Help me
exclaim like Mary, "He lives, he lives"!
I see. I believe. I live. Thank you, Jesus. Amen.

Bible verse: "And he said to them, 'Go into all the world and proclaim
the good news to the whole creation.' " Mark 16:15

Division 3: Passion, Mark 8:31—16:20
Unit 14: Crucifixion and Resurrection, Mark 15:16—16:20
Paragraph 1: The Mockery, Mark 15:16-20

Study verses 16-20 and record five observations.
Who had been standing by, ready to stop any uprising?
What is a cohort? Refer to a Bible dictionary or encyclopedia if needed.
Find twelve verbs of action that describe the mockery and brutality
of the Roman soldiers and write them in your notebook.
What did a purple robe and a crown signify?
Do you think any of the Roman soldiers objected to this gruesome
ordeal?

Did they mock Jesus because of boredom, fear, or unbelief, or were they just completing their job?

Today's challenge:
Imagine Jesus' human condition following the strenuous days and sleepless nights. Only the Holy Spirit can reveal the human suffering Jesus endured for you and me. Jesus can identify with each of us so beautifully. Do you carry pain from your childhood, school days, or marriage? Were you mistreated, loved less than your siblings, or abandoned? Are you handicapped, poor, or discriminated against because of your race? Jesus, the wounded Servant, understands! He wants to touch and heal those deep hurts.

Write today's challenge as a prayer:

Other prayers:

Questions for discussion or reflection:
When have you audibly or by action mocked Jesus?
What would you have done if you had been Pilate? The soldiers? The disciples?
How many steps are there in the humiliation of Christ? (See the Leader's Guide.)

LESSON 94

Pray the prayer and review the Bible verse from Lesson 93.

Division 3: Passion, Mark 8:31—16:20
Unit 14: Crucifixion and Resurrection, Mark 15:16—16:20
Paragraph 2: Golgotha, Mark 15:21-24
Paragraph 3: The Crucifixion, Mark 15:25-32

Study verses 21-32 and record five observations.
Who is "they" Mark referred to?
Who was Simon? What do we know about him?

Why didn't the soldiers help Jesus carry the cross?
Note how Mark summarized what the soldiers did with Jesus.
Why wouldn't Jesus take the wine?
How was Scripture fulfilled by the way soldiers divided up Jesus' clothes? (Ps. 22:18)
Do you remember when Jesus was first called the King of the Jews?
Why was the inscription *The King of the Jews* ironic? (John 19:19-22)
Twice, those who derided Jesus ignorantly spoke the truth about him. What did they say?

Today's challenge:
Record all the acts of humiliation Jesus suffered on the cross. In what ways have you humiliated Jesus?

Write today's challenge as a prayer:

Other prayers:

Questions for discussion or reflection:
What symbolism do you see in the vertical and horizontal bars that make up the cross?
What is the irony of Jesus' being crucified between robbers?
How does this humiliation of Jesus strike you?
What should be our response to the cross?
How could you prove that this was the greatest act of love ever given?

LESSON 95

Pray the prayer and review the Bible verse from Lesson 93.

Division 3: Passion, Mark 8:31—16:20
Unit 14: Crucifixion and Resurrection, Mark 15:16—16:20
Paragraph 4: Death, Mark 15:33-39
Paragraph 5: The Women, Mark 15:40-41

Study 15:33-41 and record five observations. Refer to a Bible encyclopedia to learn how the Jews measured time.

What happened at noon (sometimes called the sixth hour)?
What happened at 3:00 (the ninth hour)?
What did the darkness signify?
What did Jesus become during those three dark hours? (2 Cor. 5:21, Gal. 3:13)
To realize how deeply Jesus knew this darkness, read Psalm 22 and Mark 14:36.
How did Jesus break the darkness and silence?
Why did Mark use Aramaic words?
Why did the Father have to forsake his Son?
Do you think Jesus suffered more physically or spiritually?
For further light on verse 37, turn to John 19:30.

Why was the curtain torn in two when Jesus died? (Matt. 27:51-54; Heb. 9:6-12; 10:19-22)
Imagine what the priests saw when Jesus died (Matt. 27:51). What did the centurion see?
Read Paragraph 5, Mark 15:40-41, again. Imagine the heart rending feelings of these women!
Write the names mentioned in your notebook.
What love and compassion was yearning in their hearts?
What do you think they wanted to do?
How did God understand their hopelessness?

Today's challenge:
How do you identify with the centurion?
In what way were you and I present at the crucifixion?
How has Jesus' shed blood kept death from our door?
Do you live as if God understands your joys, trials, and hopelessness?

Write today's challenge as a prayer:

Other prayers:

Questions for discussion or reflection:
What curtain separates you from God?
How did Christ die for the people in your home, church, community?
How are you helping the wounded hearts in your neighborhood and church—those with fractured relationships, spiritual vacuums, gnawing worry over cancer or other illnesses? Can you form a small support group, have a troubled person over for coffee, spend time praying specifically?

131

LESSON 96

Be still before God as you pray the prayer and review the Bible verse from Lesson 93.

Division 3: Passion, Mark 8:31—16:20
Unit 14: Crucifixion and Resurrection, Mark 15:16—16:20
Paragraph 6: Burial, Mark 15:42-47

Study 15:42-47 and record five observations. This was the evening of the crucifixion, the evening of the Day of Preparation.
What did Mark tell us about Joseph? List four things in your notebook.
Find out how long it normally took a body to die on a cross.
Why did Jesus' sudden death alarm Pilate?
Why did Joseph want to take Jesus' body off the cross so soon? (Deut. 21:22-23)
What risks did Joseph take when he asked for Jesus' body?
How did Joseph prepare Jesus' body for burial? List five things in your notebook.
Who helped Joseph? (John 19:39)

Imagine the grief and sorrow of these men as they pulled out the spikes in Jesus' hands and feet and saw the ugly marks of pain. No doubt Jesus' face was caked with blood and covered with black-and-blue marks from the cruel blows!
Why is verse 47 so important?

Today's challenge:
When have you taken courage like Joseph?
What in your life holds you entombed—fear, worry, pride, jealousy, greed?

Write today's challenge as a prayer:

Other prayers:

Questions for discussion or reflection:
How did Jesus' death change the world? Your world?
Who brought the gospel to you or your ancestors? How grateful are you?

LESSON 97

Pray the prayer and review the Bible verse from Lesson 93.

Division 3: Passion, Mark 8:31—16:20
Unit 14: Crucifixion and Resurrection, Mark 15:16—16:20
Paragraph 7: The Resurrection, Mark 16:1-8

Study 16:1-8 and record five observations.
What day of the week was the Sabbath?
Notice that the same three women who witnessed Jesus' death are mentioned. Why didn't they anoint Jesus?
What day, where, and when did they go to anoint him?
Why did they go before?
What thoughts raced through the women's minds as they saw the empty tomb?
Read the angel's message, taking special note of the verbs! What was the angel's most amazing statement?
Why was special mention made of Peter? (Mark 14:72)
Record the vivid words Mark used to describe the women as they left the tomb.
What did Mark mean by "they said nothing"?

Today's challenge:
Notice the command "Go, tell." To believe something you must tell it! Name a thrilling experience you've had that was difficult to explain to others. How do you know Jesus' resurrection is true?

Write today's challenge as a prayer:

Other prayers:

Questions for discussion or reflection:
Who first told you about Jesus' resurrection?
How did you come to believe it?
The Bible says, "Go, tell." Whom have you told? Whom are you telling?
Are you living as if it's "Friday" or "Sunday"?

LESSON 98

Pray the prayer and review the Bible verse from Lesson 93. Let its truth burn into your heart.

Division 3: Passion, Mark 8:31—16:20
Unit 14: Crucifixion and Resurrection, Mark 15:16—16:20
Paragraph 8: First Appearance, Mark 16:9-11
Paragraph 9: Second Appearance, Mark 16:12-13
Paragraph 10: Go, Tell, Mark 16:14-18

Study 16:9-18 and record five observations. The closing verses of Mark are often disputed, but I can't imagine Mark not finishing his Gospel. Notice how verse 15 underscores 1:1.
When did Jesus rise?
Why do you think Jesus appeared to Mary Magdalene first?
Imagine how afraid and excited Mary was. What did she do immediately? (John 20:1-3)
Why wouldn't or couldn't the disciples believe Mary?
How do you think Mary felt when they wouldn't believe her message?

Read Paragraph 9, Mark 16:12-13, again. Then read Luke 24:13-35. Isn't this exciting? Try to be like a child as you read it.
What do you think "another form" means?
How did Mark emphasize the disciples' confusion?

Read Paragraph 10, Mark 16:14-18, again.

Now to whom did Jesus appear?

For what did Jesus reprimand his disciples?

Mark quickly included Jesus' final command. What is the believer's tremendous task?

What does "believe" mean to you?

What does "be saved" mean?

How is the universality of God's grace expressed?

Underline the word *believe*. What does the word *condemned* mean?

What tremendous powers and signs are given to those who truly believe? List five powers in your notebook.

Wherein lies the power for these signs? (Mark 9:37-41)

Do you believe the power is yours?

Today's challenge:

What is your reaction to these events?

Read John 20:1-18. This is so exciting! Why did John believe?

What would your reaction have been if you had been there?

Write today's challenge as a prayer:

Other prayers:

Questions for discussion or reflection:

Do you know *about* Jesus or do you *know* him? How?

Are you afraid of the phrase *be saved* today?

Has it become trite?

How do you "go" into all the world?

When last did you experience the power Jesus promised?

LESSON 99

Pray the prayer and review the Bible verse from Lesson 93. Underline the two verbs in the command.

Division 3: Passion, Mark 8:31—16:20
Unit 14: Crucifixion and Resurrection, Mark 15:16—16:20
Paragraph 11: The Ascension, Mark 16:19-20

Study verses 19-20 and record five observations.
Where did this take place? (Luke 24:50-51)
Jesus, the Servant, now became "Lord." What does the name *Lord Jesus* mean to you?
What was Jesus' last command to his disciples? (Matt. 28:16-20)
What does the right hand of God signify?
How excited were Jesus' followers following his ascension?
What did they do?
What did the Lord do?
Verse 20 says "while the Lord worked with them." Can we also experience that blessing?

Today's challenge:
How do you feel when you read this power-packed paragraph?
What benefit do we have from Christ's presence at the right hand of the Father?
How are we living and writing the gospel today?
How can we keep the gospel message alive?

Write today's challenge as a prayer:

Other prayers:

Questions for discussion or reflection:
How can we daily live in the power of the resurrection?
What new message has come to you through Christ's glorious resurrection?
Are you excited about heaven?
To whom has Jesus sent you?
How has Jesus confirmed your message? Be specific!

LESSON 100

Be still in adoration before God. Pray the prayer and review all the
Bible verses.

When my husband, Merrill, taught the Gospel of Mark at Waldorf
College, most of his students could write from memory the names of
the three divisions, fourteen units, and all 124 paragraphs by the end
of the study! Is the structure of this Gospel as clear in your mind?

Today review the whole Gospel of Mark—focusing first on the three
divisions (see the outline on pages 10 and 11).

Why did Mark devote half of his Gospel to only one week in Jesus'
life, his passion?

What historical significance does the last week of Jesus' life on earth
encompass?

Mark swept through Jesus' life in brilliancy and passion and plead with
the Romans and with us to see this Jesus, this Lord. Can't you see the
signs that follow those who believe?

Now review the units. Striking, aren't they?

Did you know we had a Gospel that so logically portrayed Jesus' life?

Have you memorized the Bible verses?

The key verse (Mark 10:45) has been fulfilled: he *came*, he *served*, he
died. Slowly repeat the key verse.

Do you see how this verse fits into the three divisions—Preparation,
Proclamation, and Passion?

Today's challenge:
Close your eyes and see this "beginning" of the Gospel (Mark 16:20).
How the Romans and others must have thrilled to have Mark's powerful,
action-filled Gospel in their hands! Who is continuing this Gospel now?
Are you? Go forth in the name of Jesus!

137

Write today's challenge as a prayer:

Other prayers:

Questions for discussion or reflection:
You will be blessed continually as you give the Word to others. With whom can you study this Gospel? Your family? A friend? A group? Your church?

Words make things happen. In Gen. 1:3 God says, "Let there be light," and there was light. Rom. 10:10 says that one confesses with the mouth and so is saved! "Go, tell"—we must release the power of Jesus. Mark began with "the beginning of the good news"—now he has given us Jesus' Word to continue it: *"Go, tell."*

LEADER'S GUIDE

This brief leader's guide provides help for the leader of a Bible study group or for the individual searcher. It gives more information on some points in the lesson, reflects further on the meaning of the passage, provides answers for the more difficult questions, and suggests a prayer thought to close the lesson. Most of the prayer thoughts are from *Prayer* by O. Hallesby; the page numbers refer to the 1975 edition.

Please do not refer to this guide until you have thoroughly studied the section from Mark for the day. From your own study, you will find out what the Holy Spirit has in store for you!

LESSON 1

Did you underline the verbs in the opening prayer? Did you notice the verbs in the Bible verse as you read it aloud? Where did you display the verse?

When we receive a letter, we like to know something about the writer. So as we begin our study, let's see what we can learn about the author of the Gospel of Mark—not what people say, but what the Bible says about him.

John Mark's father was probably dead because he is not mentioned. Mark's mother, Mary, evidently a woman of wealth, must have been a devout Christian woman. She was a woman of prominence and influence whose heart overflowed with love and compassion for Jesus' flock. Imagine the risk she took in welcoming this large group within her home during this period of danger. Herod had already killed James (Acts 12:1), so Mark must have known the danger of the situation. Yet Mary's reputation in the Christian community was well established: Peter knew where to go to notify his friends of his miraculous deliverance.

Mark must have been personally acquainted with the circumstances surrounding Jesus' life and death—the joy, sorrows, fears, and bravery.

Mark himself was a terrific author! He was talented, yes. But he let the Holy Spirit use his talent to make the life of Christ move before us in awe, action, and exquisite majesty.

Prayer thought: Remember, prayer is hard work. Three forces seek to hinder us—the devil, the world, and our own flesh! God is round about us in Christ on every hand, with his many-sided and all-sufficient grace.[1] (*Prayer*, p. 12)

LESSON 2

Are the opening prayer and Bible verse becoming more meaningful to you?

Can you imagine Peter leaning on young Mark as they journeyed over hill and vale and by land and sea? Do you think the journeys became easier as Peter repeated the stirring stories about Jesus until Mark could actually see the scenes recorded so vividly in his Gospel? Do you think Peter at times wiped away a tear or poured out his heart to Mark as he told him about his failures, denials, and doubts? Use your imagination as you study this fiery Gospel so you will fully understand its strength and majesty. It is believed Mark stayed in Rome with Peter and might have been there when Peter gave his life for his Lord. Peter mentioned Mark by name in his letter (1 Pet. 5:13).

Read the following verses to enrich your knowledge of Mark, the Gospel writer.

Col. 4:10: What a rich heritage to have a solid, unselfish, steadfast cousin like Barnabas.

Acts 12:25: It's interesting to note that apparently Mark had been with the other missionaries in Antioch.

Acts 13:2-5: Do you think Mark was present in verses 2-3? If so, what an experience that must have been! In verse 5b, Mark had the great privilege of helping Paul and Barnabas.

Acts 13:13: Maybe Mark couldn't take it. Anyway, he turned back.

Acts 15:36-40: Faithful Barnabas saw great possibilities in Mark. Perhaps Barnabas thought he had done all he could for Paul, and the Holy Spirit directed Barnabas to help Mark. What a gift of grace!

2 Tim. 4:11: Don't you love this verse? Mark again won Paul's love; shortly before his death, Paul needed Mark.

2 Tim. 4:11 and Philemon 123-24: Mark had the opportunity of knowing Luke. What do you think Luke and Mark talked about as Paul, then a prisoner, ministered to his visitors? I like to think the intellectual Dr. Luke said, "Mark, I'm researching and writing the Gospel for the Greeks. So many people—especially the Romans—need to hear that Jesus' passion in life was to go to the cross. They need to know that salvation is for them too. Write a Gospel, Mark! Make it short, full of action and love." And Mark took up the challenge!

Mark and Luke weren't the only ones to commit teaching about the gospel to writing. Here are the books written by Mark's friends:

Peter:	1 and 2 Peter	2
Luke:	Gospel of Luke, Acts	2
Paul:	Romans, 1 and 2 Corinthians	3
	Galatians, Ephesians, Philippians,	
	Colossians	4
	1 and 2 Thessalonians	2
	1 and 2 Timothy, Titus, Philemon	2
	Total books by Mark's friends:	17

Prayer thought: All Jesus needs is access. He enters in . . . wherever he is not denied admittance. (*Prayer*, p. 12)

LESSON 3

Did you really pray the prayer and read the Bible verse?

Mark 10:45 is the all-inclusive key verse that ties the whole book together. To better understand its meaning, turn to John 1:14. This verse helps reveal the deep significance of *the Son of Man*. Pray that the Holy Spirit will show you its meaning. Jesus is the only one who uses the name *the Son of Man* in Mark's Gospel. (The word *for* in Mark 10:45 says look back, and the word *but* says look ahead.)

On our first trip to New York, we entered the city on the Fourth of July. We were overwhelmed! How would we ever find our way around? Wisely, a pastor friend had told us, "Go to the top of the Empire State Building. Get an overview of the avenues, streets, Hudson

River, and all. Have no fear, you'll get it." We followed his advice, and we did understand the layout of the city!

In a similar way, Mark 10:45 gives an overview of the Gospel of Mark. To further our study, we'll divide the Gospel into three parts that correspond to the three verbs in our key verse. This is the Son of Man's program!

Preparation	Proclamation	Passion
(to come)	(to serve)	(to give)
1:1-13	1:14—8:30	8:31—16:20

In your Bible, write "Preparation" at 1:1, "Proclamation" at 1:14, and "Passion" at 8:31.

The word *ransom* brings forth the picture of a slave. Do you remember *Uncle Tom's Cabin* by Harriet Beecher Stowe?

Prayer thought: As air enters in quietly when we breathe, and does its normal work in our lungs, so Jesus enters quietly into our hearts and does his blessed work there. (*Prayer*, p. 12)

LESSON 4

Mark 1:1, Greatest Title

Mark's introduction of Jesus is brief, compact, and to the point. There is no mention of Jesus' birth, genealogy, or infancy as there is in the Gospels of Matthew or Luke. Many people to whom Mark was writing may have known the story of Jesus' life and were not interested in Jesus' "roots." Therefore, Mark launched right into action.

In the first sentence, Mark gave his readers a mouthful. He promised to tell an exciting story—a true one! If you'd never read it before, you'd find it to be more fascinating than a popular novel!

Remember, this is the beginning of the gospel, a new beginning, but not the beginning of Jesus Christ (John 17:5).

Why did Mark specifically say "Jesus Christ, the Son of God"? "Jesus" is a personal name. It was a common name among Jews of that day (Col. 4:11). It is still used in Mexico, Spain, and Portugal. "Christ," however, is an official title. It is the Greek word for "Messiah." The Messiah, or "the Anointed One," was to restore Israel. To Jews, the word *Messiah* meant salvation. They had been looking for the promised Messiah for hundreds of years. So Mark was saying that Jesus wasn't only a man with a human name, wasn't only the Christ—Messiah of the race—but was the very Son of God. In fact, he was one with God (John 1:1; 10:30). Our human minds can't possibly grasp the truth! Many gods were worshiped in Rome, but Mark wanted his readers to know the one, true Son of God.

The Greatest Title (the name of the first paragraph) contains a tremendous explanation of the Gospel of Mark! I hope you sensed Mark's excitement! The gospel is still good news!

Prayer thought: To pray is nothing more involved than to let Jesus into our needs. (*Prayer*, 12)

LESSON 5

Mark 1:2-8, Greatest Forerunner

As you study Mark 1:2-8, keep in mind that John was the first speaking prophet in Israel for more than four hundred years—since the day of Malachi. Some thought John might be the Messiah, the Christ (Luke 3:15).

God had promised Isaiah that he would send a deliverer. Why was John sent before Jesus? It was customary at that time to send messengers or forerunners to prepare the way for a king. An announcer always preceded an important Roman official. The roads were few, and often in need of repair. Hence, workers were sent ahead to level, to prepare, and to mend the way, making the important person's paths straight. What paths did John have to make straight? The wilderness of sin had made Jesus' paths crooked and hilly. John, by preaching on the forgiveness of sins and baptism, helped to level the paths, plow down the hills of unbelief and superstition, and fill in the valleys of doubt and fear. The paths? The paths of people's hearts, full of evil, needed the plow of repentance.

Could John level these paths and make them straight? No, he was only the voice, only a messenger, but he had the wonderful privilege of pointing to One, the Servant. With such an interesting forerunner, certainly the one who was coming must be special!

Notice how picturesquely Mark placed the Servant on the scene. The desert here is truly theological as well as geographical. John the Baptist closed off the old age; Christ opened the new age! When Jesus baptizes an individual with the Holy Spirit, the whole person is transformed. The Holy Spirit, the Spirit of Jesus, lives within that person. God truly had not forgotten his promise recorded in Isaiah! The Savior was at hand!

Answers to questions about Mark 1:2-3: "I" is God; the "messenger" is John; "you" is Jesus; the messenger will prepare the way; John's "voice" will cry out.

John's message was repentance. Repentance means to take a good look at yourself—your desires, choices, friends, and interests. Repent means to turn around! Go the other way! The best way to change is to *look at Jesus*!

Prayer thought: To pray is to let Jesus glorify his name in the midst of our needs. (*Prayer*, p. 13)

LESSON 6

Mark 1:9-11, Greatest Confirmation

Nazareth was a small town in the province of Galilee (Matt. 2:22-23). Many Roman troops resided there. Zealous Jews hated the Romans for making them pay taxes. Often, the soldiers had little respect for the Jews as well. Hence, the little town of Nazareth was despised.

The Jewish people of that time mourned the loss of the prophets. For four hundred years God had been silent! Imagine the excitement when, at Jesus' baptism, the heavens tore open and a voice from heaven spoke and a Spirit appeared!

Did you notice how much Mark recorded in one paragraph about Jesus' baptism? Something glorious was happening here. Jesus was there in person. The Father was there in the voice, giving identification, confirmation, and assurance through his words, "This is my Son." The Holy Spirit was there in the form of a dove, empowering and guiding the Son. Here we have the powerful Trinity in action.

Is the powerful Trinity a part of your life? Thank God for a church that emphasizes the Trinity (2 Cor. 13:14).

Jesus did not need baptism for cleansing, but by this humble act he was inaugurated into his mighty office of Prophet, High Priest, and King. He was truly identified as the Son of God, the Messiah to come.

Prayer thought: To pray is nothing more involved than to lie in the sunshine of his grace. (*Prayer*, p. 15)

LESSON 7

Mark 1:12-13, Greatest Confrontation

In one sentence, Mark portrayed the Servant's life: He will be empowered by the Spirit, opposed by Satan and his forces, given command by God over all creation, and attended by angels. No one could have written this unless he were inspired by the Holy Spirit.

Mark's introduction of Jesus was brief because he wanted to get on with this Servant's dynamic ministry. But to identify with all of us, Jesus had to face Satan's temptations. Remember, being tempted is not sin—giving in to temptation is sin! What an example Jesus was in combating temptation with the Word (Matt. 4:1-11, Luke 4:1-13)! What a Helper we have. He knows our trials!

This concludes the first division, Jesus' Preparation (see pages 10 and 11). Notice that the first unit covers the same verses as the first division. It's short, but sufficient for Gentiles and Romans who liked power, action, strength, and glory and were not as interested in Christ's lineage as the Jews were. Therefore, the Beginning needed just four short paragraphs. After the title, Mark had to show the Gentiles that Jesus was a King, so he introduced the forerunner, John the Baptist. Then he had to show that Jesus was officially inaugurated into his ministry by the Almighty Father and sealed by the Holy Spirit in baptism. In almost every paragraph of Mark's Gospel we will notice the dark background of evil. So Jesus had to face Satan, the source of all evil. With this brief, but powerful background, Mark had set the stage for Jesus to begin his ministry.

Can you name the four paragraphs? Also try writing the four most important events in your life.

Prayer thought: To be a man or woman of prayer is . . . to give Jesus, with his wonder-working power, access to our distress night and day. (*Prayer*, p. 15)

LESSON 8

Mark 1:14-15, Repent, Believe

Remember, Mark's Gospel has three clear, concise divisions—Preparation, Proclamation, and Passion. We finished the short first division, Preparation. Now we begin the second division, Proclamation. We also begin the second unit, Growing Popularity. The first paragraph of this unit is Mark 1:14-15.

Mark's objective was to present the public ministry of Jesus. So he omitted events of the one and one-half years between Jesus' temptation and the arrest of John the Baptist. He used the word *now* to cover those years. Mark provided no background about Jesus or John, so we assume his readers must have known something about them. Mark's gift of brevity is fascinating, for it includes significant, powerful information. Thus, the reader progresses through the chapters from one climax to another, all leading up to the final climax. It is fascinating to follow the rapid-moving panorama of events.

The three provinces of Palestine in Jesus' day were Judea, Samaria, and Galilee. Look at the map on page 240. At this time in his ministry, Jesus stayed away from the argumentative crowds in Jerusalem. Instead he went to Galilee—to the lonely and the hungry. He went to ordinary folks like you and me.

We can see how Jesus took Galilee by storm. Notice Jesus' actions, and the people's reaction. Mark sought to present the Preacher through word and deed. Notice that Jesus presented himself as a Servant with a message—not as a healer with miracles. The message—repentance—was the same as that of John the Baptist, but Jesus added one more aspect to the message: believe! Repent and believe seems to be a command, for this is what brings the kingdom of God into our hearts. Isn't it wonderful that we don't have to possess fame, riches, or fortune to belong to the kingdom? All we need is a helpless, confessing, believing heart!

Reread Jesus' awe-inspiring gospel in verse 15. What a new beginning! What a gift! What good news! Jesus began his message by saying, "The time is fulfilled." Alexander the Great had swept across the world and introduced one language, Greek. Rome had conquered the world, so there was peace. The Greeks were intellectually confused. The Hebrews were longing for the Messiah. God had prepared the world with one language, a time of peace, and a longing for the Messiah.

To satisfy this longing, the heavens opened at Jesus' baptism, and the kingdom of God—the good news, the gospel—arrived in the person of Jesus. Repentance was the key. Believing in the bearer of the message would satisfy the longing. In Greek, the word *believe* means action. Our world is hungry for repentance. It longs for assurance of life in Jesus! Pray that you might have a longing for repentance and believe the good news Mark proclaimed.

Mark used the present tense extensively in his Gospel, and that gives movement and vigor. He often used the words *and, immediately, now,* or *as soon as.* Notice that *and* or action words begin the sentences in verses 17, 18, 20, 23, 24, 26, and 28.

Prayer thought: Prayer is something deeper than words. . . . Prayer is an attitude of our hearts, an attitude of mind. (*Prayer*, p. 16)

LESSON 9

Mark 1:16-20, Follow Me

Pinpoint the Sea of Galilee on your map (page 240) to see its relationship to other well-known places in Palestine. Notice that the brothers followed Jesus immediately. They weren't professional men, but ordinary workers. Did you notice that two were casting their nets, and the others were repairing their nets? Did you notice that the parents of James and John had hired servants?

Close your eyes and envision the scene, and Jesus' tremendous love and popularity. When Jesus came, God's kingdom began to become visible. According to John 1:35-42, this was not the first time these brothers had seen Jesus. They had previous contact with him and had come to know and trust him. In this paragraph, Mark merely recorded Jesus' official call to them.

Do not view the brothers' response lightly. Think of the separation and sacrifice Jesus' call entailed. It was tremendous! Following Jesus does not require the same sacrifice from each of us, but it does demand obedience and a commitment to spending time with him. Obedience is vitally important, so we don't quench the Holy Spirit. If we don't obey, we may not feel the nudge of the Holy Spirit as clearly in the future (1 Thess. 5:19).

Prayer thought: Prayer and helplessness are inseparable. Only a person who is helpless can truly pray. (*Prayer*, p. 17)

LESSON 10

Mark 1:21-28, With Authority

Capernaum was a major fishing village and headquarters for the Roman troops. It boasted great wealth, but also much sin and evil. Hence, the good news was needed both for the Jews and the Romans. Jesus moved to Capernaum from Nazareth (Matt. 4:12-13).

> The rulers of the synagogue must have asked Jesus to teach. During the Babylonian exile of 70 years, the Jews felt the need of coming together to talk over the things of God, and to pray for their deliverance and restoration to the homeland. The Sabbath day was the logical time for this. At first homes were probably used for meeting places. Later special buildings were erected for this purpose. They were called synagogues. Remember the temple was in Jerusalem.[2]

No permanent rabbi was provided, so visiting teachers were often asked to read the scroll and teach. Jesus' authority in preaching was marvelous compared to the scribes, interpreters of the Old Testament laws, who merely quoted authorities. Plus, Jesus' authority over demons was astounding. Remember that the Romans were people of courage, but imagine how demonology puzzled them. People were awed by Jesus' message and stood in wonder and reverence at his power. Wherever his Word is proclaimed, there is power, and Mark continues to proclaim that divine power in word and deed. For isn't this the new beginning, the gospel which will heal each one of us from the evil that disrupts our lives?

The Sabbath, from sunset Friday to sunset Saturday, was the Jewish day of rest. The beauty of Jesus, recognizing the captivity of this human being is astounding to the crowd and also to us!

What are six characteristics of demons or unclean spirits? A demon is an evil spirit within a person; a demon has command over a person's physical being; a demon recognizes the deity of Christ; a demon is fearful of the presence of Christ, but seems to be drawn to Christ; a demon loses in Christ's presence. Even the underworld recognizes the Messiah's authority. That is why the demon was reluctant to leave this world and be cast into the abyss.

Jesus proved his authority over demons by causing them to be silent. Jesus wanted to be known as the Son of God. Miracles were important, but teaching his divine message must come first—and not according to Satan's timetable.

The crowd should not have asked, "What is this?" but "Who is this?" What the crowd witnessed was not an event, but a person—Jesus! The person of Jesus spells power, strength, majesty! When I was a teenager, and even now, the words our pastor used at Holy Communion thrilled me—"By the authority of God and my holy office I declare unto you the gracious forgiveness of all your sins in the name of the Father, Son, and Holy Spirit." What joy! What strength!

Prayer thought: God becomes actively engaged at once in hearing and answering the prayer of your helplessness. (*Prayer*, p. 17)

LESSON 11

Mark 1:29-31, Simon's Mother-in-Law

Think about Jesus' availability, his sense of mission, and his steadfast purpose. How exhausted he must have been! Certainly Peter (also called Simon in John 1:42) had been astounded at Jesus' power over the unclean spirit.

Peter was married, and his mother-in-law lived in his home. Notice Jesus' love in the words *came and took her by the hand and lifted her up*. She needed no time to recuperate, but got up and served others. What good news we are seeing! What a comfort this can be to those who are aged or on sick beds. Imagine Jesus coming in, gently taking your hands, and saying, "Peace I leave with you; my peace I give to you. I do not give to you as the world gives. Do not let your hearts be troubled, and do not let them be afraid" (John 14:27). "And if I go and prepare a place for you, I will come again and will take you to myself" (John 14:3a). Dwelling on this lovely scene might help us live above our pain and rejoice in his coming to take us home! Relax in Jesus' comfort!

This observation from a missionary reminds us that God is still in the business of healing:

> One day they gave me the privilege of watching a cataract surgery. What a fascinating procedure! It was exciting to see the tremendous skill of the Lord given to the surgeon. Surely our Lord Jesus is still in the business of healing and restoring sight to the blind, often through the hands of a doctor. I'll never forget the blind 89-year-old woman pausing at the door of the operating room, eyes wide open and giving thanks to the Lord.[3]

Prayer thought: Infants cannot formulate in words a single petition to you. Yet the little ones pray the best way they know how. All they can do is cry, but you understand their pleading. (*Prayer*, pp. 17, 18)

LESSON 12

Mark 1:32-34, Sunset Scene

This was the Sabbath (sunset Friday to sunset Saturday), and Jewish leaders had proclaimed that no healing take place on the Sabbath (Luke 13:14).

The Jews had two distinct evening times: The first was from 3:00 to 6:00 and the second was after that, at sundown. With the Sabbath ending at sundown, the people could begin bringing sufferers to Jesus without violating the Sabbath rules. The report of Jesus' marvelous healing in the synagogue had apparently spread like wildfire!

Demon possession was not considered a sickness, because it is mentioned separately, with the conjunction *and*. Jesus would not let the demons speak and proclaim their spiritual knowledge, because he knew they would not give the right testimony. Furthermore, Jesus did not want to be proclaimed the Messiah yet. His time had not yet come. Satan wanted the crowds to follow Jesus because he was popular. Jesus wanted to be followed because he was the Son of God, the Messiah! Mark's Gospel really teaches the reality of the spiritual world.

Most assuredly demons exist in the world today! With the influence of cults and satanic forces, we need the comfort provided in Scripture through passages like Eph. 6:10-13; Col. 2:8, 15; and John 10:27-30; 14:30; and 16:33.

Prayer thought: God is forever occupied with hearing this prayer of ours and satisfying all our needs. (*Prayer*, p. 18)

LESSON 13

Mark 1:35-39, Sunrise Scene

Galilee was the northernmost province of Palestine. It was approximately sixty miles long and thirty miles wide. There were more than two hundred towns in Galilee. Hence, it was a wonderful place for Jesus to carry on his work.

Peter's balloon of pride must have burst when Jesus informed him that his mission was to "go on to the neighboring towns"!

Try to keep in mind that Jesus' days were long and strenuous, but his constant communion with his Father gave his actions authority and power! Each day, Jesus fulfilled his mission. That is why he continued throughout Galilee, preaching and casting out demons.

Notice the verbs in Jesus' answer. He refuted the temptation of popularity by stating a fact, "So that I may proclaim the message there also; for that is what I came out to do." What masterful control!

I like to meditate on the contrast between Christ's pressing activity in the first verses of this chapter and his quiet escape for prayer in the latter verses. We must not forget that Jesus was human too! Taking time to be alone with the Father gave Jesus direction and power. No wonder he was in absolute command in every situation—preaching, healing, and sending his joy throughout all of Galilee with no irritation or hurry. This Servant—who had full command over demons and physical disease, who had surprised everyone with his ability to preach with authority, and whose popularity had risen to such heights that everyone came to see him—still needed to draw away for prayer. Jesus went; he preached; he cast out demons. How foolish we are to think we can work without prayer!

Prayer thought: Your prayer is a result of the fact that Jesus has knocked at your heart's door and told you that he desires to gain access to your needs. (*Prayer*, p. 20)

LESSON 14

Mark 1:40-45, Loving the Unlovable

The Roman soldiers were powerful—at least Rome thought so. However, demon possession and leprosy left Rome's most powerful in a state of utter helplessness. But Mark's Servant stood fearless in the face of these horrors.

Leprosy was a gruesome, horrible disease. A leper became an outcast, forced to live apart, outside the village—absolutely hopeless! A leper was required to wear a chin covering and shout the warning "Unclean, unclean" when in public.

Have you ever imagined how this leper got to Jesus? Did some dear relatives hide him from sight until Jesus was very near? Can you imagine the leper breathlessly running toward Jesus and yelling "Unclean, unclean" so that everyone would get out of his way? Can you imagine the leper falling at the feet of Jesus, the reservoir of divine power? Imagine the awe that fell over the crowd as Jesus touched the leper— what person had ever dared to touch this man? You can almost hear the crowd gasping, "Oh, no!"

Theologians make much of the issue "that Jesus could no longer go into a town openly" following this incident, but Mark wrote a beautiful picture of what happened next. Mark said he "stayed out in the country; and people came to him from every quarter." Nothing stops Jesus, the all-encompassing Savior!

Notice, too, that Jesus sent the leper to the priest to be examined and to give an offering of thanks at the temple. Jesus always obeyed the laws of Moses. If the leper had gone to the priest, that, too, would prove Jesus' tremendous miracle!

We have completed Unit 2, Growing Popularity. See the master outline on pages 10 and 11.

Prayer thought: To pray is to open the door unto Jesus and admit him into your distress. (*Prayer*, p. 20)

LESSON 15

Mark 2:1-12, First Opposition

It seems that Jesus moved with his family from the small town of Nazareth to Capernaum at some time during the early part of his ministry. It is generally believed that Joseph had died and that Jesus' sisters had married.

Keep in mind that Jesus' important work was teaching and preaching in order to present God's kingdom, but that he proved his messiahship through healing and miracles. The Pharisees refused to recognize Jesus as the Messiah and opposed him at every turn. They stubbornly refused to relinquish their position and power.

The four friends of the paralytic had perfect confidence in Jesus. No obstacle would block their way! So Jesus rewarded their faith. Did you notice the two groups of people in this story—men of faith who acted in confidence and the scribes who questioned Jesus' authority?

Study verse 4 carefully and then read Luke 5:19.

The houses in the Orient were often built of stone, with a flat roof. A stairway led up from the outside so the roof was easily accessible. Luke mentions that the roof was made of tiles, meaning they dug away at the tiles and broke up the roof.[4]

> On the outside of these houses, whether of the poor or the wealthy, were built the stairs that led up to the roof. These stairs were made of stone. Here on the housetop, much of the family life was enjoyed, especially in the cool of the evening. The streets were dusty and noisy, while up here it was quiet and restful. Little wonder that the four friends of the palsied man could carry him up the outside stairway to the rooftop, remove the tiles, and lower him so that Jesus might speak those words of healing.[5]

Faith lets nothing hinder its goal.

Luke 5:17 tells us that people had come from every village in Galilee and Judea and from the city of Jerusalem. Were some of them really spies that had been sent out? Although their opposition was silent, Jesus knew what was in their hearts: Their greatest sin was unbelief. The opposers' blind error was that they refused to see anything but a mere man in this Servant. They opposed the Messiah they had been longing for. They rejected the miracles that proved his deity.

Make a special note of all the oppositions. Who opposed? (The scribes!) How did they oppose? (In their hearts.) What did they oppose? (Blasphemy, and the forgiveness of sins.)

Blasphemy was claiming that one could do something that only God had the power to do! And Jesus did what he claimed! Aren't you happy Jesus called himself the Son of Man? By this one stroke, Jesus expanded his messiahship beyond Israel. Jesus is the Son of God (John 20:31) who became man (John 1:14) and came to earth, taking on himself our human flesh.

"Rise, take up your 'task,' and walk." An old woman in our first parish told me, "If you ever get discouraged or bogged down, take up the closest work at hand. Do the laundry, pay some bills, or make a phone call. Don't sit there!" Her words made me chuckle, but they were good advice!

Prayer thought: Your helplessness is the very thing that opens wide the door to Jesus and gives him access to all your needs. (*Prayer*, p. 20)

LESSON 16

Mark 2:13-14, Call of Levi

In this paragraph Jesus calls the disciple who wrote the Gospel of Matthew (Matt. 9:9). Levi was his Aramaic name. (Mark's readers probably didn't read Greek, so the Aramaic is often used.) He was one of the tax-gatherers who were social outcasts and friends of the Roman government who often became rich at the expense of other Jewish people. Matthew (Levi) and his family were not even allowed in the synagogue.

He collected duty on goods that traveled through Capernaum, a thriving center for Roman troops and an important business community. As a customs officer, he would have been well educated and conversant in Greek. His office was probably situated at the entrance to Capernaum along the caravan route between Damascus and the East.

Jesus must have walked by Levi's office many times during his early years of ministry. He must have seen great potential in Matthew in order to choose him as a companion and one of his disciples. Could there have been a special yearning for the Messiah in Matthew's heart?

This despised outcast who gave up his lucrative profession became a blessing to his Lord and to the world. He wrote a Gospel and won an imperishable crown of fame and glory. His story is an abiding testimony to the power of Christ, who transformed a despised publican into an apostle, an evangelist, and a saint.

In Paragraph 1 of this unit, the people saw physical healing, but in this paragraph they see a day-by-day spiritual healing in Levi's life.

Prayer thought: "You do not know now what I am doing, but later you will understand." (John 13:7) We do not see the answer immediately. (*Prayer*, p. 21)

LESSON 17

Mark 2:15-17, Second Opposition

Did you notice that Matthew had a large home and great wealth? Did you notice the kind of people he invited to his feast? This was not a farewell feast, but a beginning. Matthew was really stepping out!

Christ's call is not for those who think they are good, but for those who need help. Jesus didn't associate with sinners because he enjoyed the society of depressed people, but because he loved them and sought to heal them. Regardless of the opposition, we must never cease from bringing others to Christ in prayer and deed, for this is God's will. Matthew had made a clean break, a public confession in word and deed. He followed Jesus and brought the Lord into his home. Does your home reveal Christ's presence?

The second opposition came from the Pharisees. They didn't dare approach Jesus with their opposition but went to the disciples instead! They questioned why Jesus ate with tax collectors and sinners. Doing so made him less honorable because tax collectors and other sinners were outcasts.

Prayer thought: Thank God for the feeling of helplessness which he has given you. (*Prayer*, p. 21)

LESSON 18

Mark 2:18-20, Third Opposition, and
Mark 2:21-23, New Not Old

Keep in mind that Jesus and the disciples had just come from a feast. Perhaps some of John's disciples had been invited to the feast, too, but refused because they were fasting.

The law commanded only one fast a year (Lev. 23:27), but the Pharisees fasted twice a week (Luke 18:12). Evidently this was one of their fast days, and Jesus was feasting! Jesus did not condemn fasting (Matt. 4:2), but insisted that it be done with the right attitude of heart and mind, for the right purpose, and not to impress others.

Jesus countered the opposition with a new truth. His present ministry was a time of celebration, like a joyous wedding. Fasting would be an expression of grief or humiliation.

Jesus further explained that fresh, new wineskins would stretch with the new, fermenting wine; old, dried wineskins would burst. The Gospel of Jesus was full of new ways and new ideas. The new life given by Jesus Christ was controlled not by rules, but by motive. So "if anyone is in Christ, there is a new creation: everything old has passed away; see everything has become new" (2 Cor. 5:17).

Jesus had not come to add new patches to the old garment of Judaism, "the old cloak," but to give a new cloak of righteousness. Therefore we must discard the old cloak of works and self-righteousness, not be enslaved by rules and regulations, but step into the new cloak of Christ's righteousness. This new life must have a new way of expression. It can't fit into old wineskins and old clothing—the old forms and ceremonies of Judaism. What a teacher he is!

Jesus truly is making all things new (Rev. 21:5a)! One day, while I was studying about old wineskins, the Holy Spirit prompted me to pray that each person on my prayer list would become a new wineskin. I chuckled as God, in the days ahead, poured new ideas and challenges into their lives.

Prayer thought: Helplessness becomes the quiet, sustaining power of our prayer life. (*Prayer*, p. 24)

LESSON 19

Mark 2:23-28, Fourth Opposition

The Jews had thirty-nine rules for the Sabbath. One wonders if the laws had become more sacred than the Sabbath! When Jesus allowed his disciples to pluck grain on the Sabbath, the Pharisees thought they had found a clear case against him. But Jesus cleverly reminded them that David, whom they esteemed so highly, broke the Sabbath law because of the higher law of necessity.

The Sabbath differs from laws of morality and honesty because we are guilty of harming others if we break those laws. Why did God create the Sabbath? For *our* good! God has given us a day for spiritual and physical restoration if we allow him. Thus the Lord's Day should be used for rest, worship, and works of necessity and mercy. Think of the many works of mercy Jesus did on the Sabbath! But keep in mind Mark's Christology: Jesus, the Servant of all, is greater than the Sabbath. The Sabbath is to be a blessing for physical upbuilding and growth in spiritual strength.

One of my students from Norway wrote about the joy she received in setting the Sabbath free. The possibility of having Sundays without homework or studies—totally released for worship, rest, relaxation, and visiting the needy—was a delight to her. The mere thought of such a fun day changed her thinking patterns and schedules. She had used Sunday as a day to finish what she hadn't accomplished during the week. Now Jesus would be the Lord of her Sabbath.

The fourth opposition: By whom? (Pharisees.) How? (Said to Jesus.) For what? (His disciples plucking grain on Sabbath.)

Prayer thought: Often we slip out of this blessed attitude of help-lessness before God and into our former life of self-pride and self-sufficiency. (*Prayer*, p. 25)

LESSON 20

Mark 3:1-6, Fifth Opposition

Jesus' custom was to be in the synagogue on the Sabbath. In this fifth and last opposition, the violent critics were ready to pounce on Jesus. Although works of mercy should be performed on the Sabbath, the Pharisees' application of the law forbid doing good, but permitted evil by refusing to help others in time of need. While Jesus looked on this man in mercy, the Pharisees looked on the scene with malicious glee.

Notice Jesus' look of anger. It was one of deep concern. He was grieved by their hardness of heart. They were silent and knew they were wrong. Notice also that Jesus did not work. He did not touch the man; he only spoke four words. Even so, a climax had been reached. The Pharisees left to join hands with the Herodians, their hated enemies and friends of Rome. What unbelief!

The fifth opposition: By whom? (The accusers.) How? (Watched Jesus so they might accuse him.) Why? (For doing good on the Sabbath!) Make a chart of the five oppositions and see their growth.

> To refuse help is harm; to decline to rescue life is murder. When, therefore, one fails to show mercy on the Sabbath, he is guilty of the most extreme lowliness and of the most unpardonable desecration. The Sabbath law does require rest from labor, but that law must yield to the law of love.[6]

Did you see the progression of the Pharisees' opposition to Jesus? First they questioned in their hearts (2:6); then they "said to his disciples" (2:16); next the people "said to him" (2:18); and, finally, the Pharisees "said to him" (2:24) "so that they might accuse him" (3:2).

We have completed Unit 3, Growing Opposition, Mark 2:1—3:6.
See the outline on pages 10 and 11.

Prayer thought: "Because apart from me you can do nothing." (John
15:5b)

LESSON 21

Mark 3:7-12, Withdrawal

Now we begin Unit 4, Growing Organization. Notice the activity, feelings, and power as the majestic figure of Christ marches on. What a
tremendous unit this is! We will see the two great forces of good and
evil at work in the world. We will see how Jesus handles them and
how he helps the disciples understand these forces.

The demons, the most pitiful beings, seem to be conscious of Jesus'
power over them and are driven to yell out that Jesus is the Holy One
of God (Mark 1:24). Their witness was a proof of Jesus' power and
authority over evil. Remember, Jesus had much work to do and did
not want to be fully known at this time. Furthermore, he knew that
the demons would not give the right testimony about him. Just knowing about Jesus, like the demons did, does not guarantee salvation.
Jesus asked those who would follow him to repent and obey.

Study the map on page 240 and see how the multitudes came from
great distances. Jerusalem, Judea, and Idum were to the south, Perea
was to the east ("beyond the Jordan"), and the cities of Tyre and Sidon
were to the northwest. The whole land was excited about Jesus! Many
came for curiosity, some came to hear his message, some were looking
for a political leader, and others sought healing, but his scheming
enemies came for evidence to use against him.

Prayer thought: We will expect nothing of ourselves and therefore
bring all our difficulties and hindrances to God in prayer and this
means to open the door to him. (*Prayer*, p. 26)

LESSON 22

Mark 3:13-19a, The Twelve

What an honor and a privilege to be chosen by Jesus! Notice that in our listing of the disciples, Peter has the two sets of brothers; Philip has two disciples whose names end in "ew" plus Thomas; and James has Judas Iscariot plus Thaddeus, who is often referred to as Judas, and Simon. Jesus did not select the Twelve because they had more faith or ability than others. In fact, they were ordinary personalities with modest means. But, remember, they left all and followed Jesus, listening to him and obeying him. At the right time, these twelve men turned the course of history.

A little less than a year remains for Jesus to teach his disciples. So notice and take in the intense training Jesus offers from now on! It's tremendous training for you and me too! What a privilege we have to be witnesses for Christ; but, if we are to testify, we must first associate with the Lord. We are a blessing to others in proportion to the time we spend with him in word and deed.

Prayer thought: Another aspect of prayer is faith. "And without faith it is impossible to please God" (Heb. 11:6a). The essence of faith is to come to Christ. (*Prayer*, p. 29)

LESSON 23

Mark 3:19b-27, Head-on Collision

The scribes had walked sixty to seventy miles to accuse Jesus. Their charge that Jesus was controlled by the devil was not only unreasonable, but also sinful. They were baffled by Jesus' wisdom and authority and had seen his miracles, but they discredited his supernatural power by saying he was in league with the devil. They didn't want to believe that he had power from God, for that would point to the fact that he was the Messiah.

Jesus cleverly exposed their contradictions (verses 23-27). However, his love is incomprehensible. Despite their false accusation, he still loved the scribes and tried to win them. Jesus first faced his accusers with the obvious rhetorical question, "How can Satan cast out Satan?" Then he used three examples—a kingdom, a house, and Satan himself—to show the absurdity of their charge. He drove his point home with the example of the strong man: Only one stronger than demons could cast out demons, and only God is stronger than demons.

> Where God's Holy Spirit was, these Jews saw the devil. Where the Holy Spirit is pronounced a devil, an unclean spirit, there repentance is no longer possible. The Spirit alone works repentance, and where the Holy Spirit is rejected, His work ceases (Heb. 6:4-6).[7]

Prayer thought: Helplessness united with faith produces prayer. (*Prayer*, p. 27)

LESSON 24

Mark 3:28-30, The Unpardonable Sin

One can blaspheme against Jesus, the Father, and creation and receive forgiveness, but not against the Holy Spirit. At one time or another, most of us have feared that we have sinned against the Holy Spirit. Our greatest comfort is that if we are worried about it, then it is impossible for us to have done so. For it is only the Holy Spirit that works sorrow and repentance in a person's heart. As Martin Luther has so rightly said, "I believe that by my own reason or strength I cannot believe in Jesus Christ, my Lord, or come to him. But the Holy Spirit has called me through the Gospel, enlightened me with his gifts, and sanctified and preserved me in the true faith."[8] The Holy Spirit is a person, one with the Father and the Son.

Study 1 John 1:9. What do we have to do? What does God do? What a glorious truth! If we but confess, God is faithful—even if we confess one minute and doubt the next. God will forgive our sins and cleanse us from all unrighteousness. What a powerful verse to use against Satan! Memorize 1 John 1:9.

Prayer thought: You have more faith than you think you have. You have enough faith to pray. (*Prayer*, p. 28)

LESSON 25

Mark 3:31-35, Family of God

In the preceding paragraph, the Pharisees tried to destroy Jesus' popularity by claiming Jesus was in league with Satan. Here, his family seemed to think he was a fanatic. It is believed that Jesus was teaching on a hillside and his relatives were standing on the outside edge of the group. What a painful situation this must have been for Jesus! He could not leave his work, even if his mother and brothers thought he was working too hard and becoming off balance. The Servant's kind heart didn't want to hurt his family, but his divine mission must come first. Notice how he rose to the occasion, how he used a difficult situation to deliver one of the most treasured quotations of Scripture.

After withdrawing and choosing the Twelve, Jesus had to show the world that his family must step aside. His work and his followers were to be first. As always in different situations, Jesus brought forth an immortal truth. He spoke of more than blood ties when in divine wisdom, he proclaimed the true nature of his family—"Whoever does the will of God." Remember, God will always take charge of our feelings if we hand our will over to him!

Do you begin to grasp what a tremendous unit this is? What a servant Jesus was to call his disciples and give them such stupendous lessons. We meet the two great forces of good and evil in this section, forces that his disciples must see and understand. Did you notice the contrast between the works of the evil one and his hosts, and the beautiful family of God?

Close your eyes and review the paragraph titles, envisioning the panorama of events: Jesus' withdrawing to become organized, his careful choosing of the Twelve after a prayer session with the Father, and his opposing the evil and embracing the good in this world. It is as if Jesus stretched his arms over the whole world and said to the Twelve, "This is the family of God 'Whoever *does* the will of God is my brother, and sister, and mother.' " Remember, it is not who hopes to, wants to, plans to, or aims to, but who *does* the will of God.

We have now completed Unit 4, Growing Organization. See the outline on pages 10 and 11.

Prayer thought: Faith manifests itself clearly and plainly when sinners come into the presence of Christ with all their sins and their distress. Sinners who do this believe. (*Prayer*, p. 29)

LESSON 26

Mark 4:1-9, Receptivity of the Word

Jesus spent a great deal of time teaching and speaking in parables, challenging his listeners to discover his hidden meaning.

In answer to the question "What is the parable about?" you may have answered, "The seed" or "The sower," but that is incorrect. This parable is about the soil. Remember, a parable emphasizes one point. What was Jesus teaching about the soil? He was showing how the Word is received into the soil (the mind and heart). In other words, he was talking about the receptivity of the Word.

The disciples would soon start teaching on their own, and they needed to know the four soils they would encounter. The four different kinds of soil into which the sower casts his seed are a vivid illustration of the four different kinds of hearers. Therefore, this parable is not about the sower (bringing the gospel to people's hearts) or the seed (the Word). It is about the different hearers of the Word, the soil (hearts) the Word falls into.

The blessings (or measure) we receive are in proportion to our receptivity of the Word. When we heed the Word, our understanding will increase, our knowledge will give us direction, and our measure will multiply. The Word will change our daily lives.

Jesus has endless blessings for us each day! How do we know God's will? The Holy Spirit reveals insight to individuals who act on what they hear! Beautifully he affirms our direction through Scripture, through a friend's affirmation, or through some other circumstance. It's so exciting to truly hear the Word of God.

Prayer thought: Faith . . . sees its own need, acknowledges its own helplessness, goes to Jesus, tells him just how bad things are, and leaves everything with him. (*Prayer*, p. 29)

LESSON 27

Mark 4:10-12, Secret of the Kingdom, and
Mark 4:13-20, The Explanation

Do you like mysteries? The kingdom of God is explained as a mystery. A mystery may be difficult to understand, but as one studies it, hidden meaning will often be understood.

Verse 12 is troublesome because these Pharisees were not capable of receiving the Word.

> Persistently declining the grace and gift whenever it came to them, these people are now without it. Thus all the realities of the Kingdom are now still a mystery to them. They nullified every effort of God in Christ to bestow the heavenly gift upon them; this nullifying is the work of persistent unbelief. . . . When unbelief has advanced far enough, not only will all its seeing and hearing produce nothing; it is even God's own will that it should be so. . . . The wicked purpose of the obdurate not to believe and be saved, God is eventually compelled to make also his purpose that they shall not believe and be saved.[9]

It is the Word that multiplies in the heart. Some of us let the Word in, others let it out, some of us never let it grow up.

Consider these contemporary descriptions of the four types of soil:

Hard path—unable to take root—occupied with other thoughts and purposely closes his or her mind.

Rocky place—good soil, but no depth—the listener is excited about a sermon or Bible study, but soon forgets about it.

Thorny place—good, but contaminated—the listener allows materialism, pleasures, sports, etc., to choke out the Word.

Good ground—good, deep, well-watered—the listener acts on the Word and yields abundant fruit.

Remember, it is not we ourselves, but the Word that multiplies. So stay in the Word. Love and prayer are tremendous soil softeners (1 Corinthians 13).

Prayer thought: "Anyone who comes to me I will never drive away." (John 6:37b)

LESSON 28

Mark 4:21-25, Use of the Word

Wouldn't you chuckle if you were staying in a rustic cabin and, when asked to light a candle, your companion stuck it under a bushel? How one admires Jesus' presentation! He uses common, everyday language to present his important message. These lamps were a real comfort in the small, dark homes of Palestine.

The lamp at that time was almost like a half-hollowed egg. On one end there was a handle and on the other end an opening through which the wick passed. The hollow egg part held the oil. When a servant brought it into a room it was put upon a stand so the small light might shed its beams. The lamp burned all night even in the poorest homes. The wick was made of twisted strands of cotton or flax and was put into the saucer of oil.[10]

Our lamps are lighted by the Word, and that's why Jesus has given us "light" to give to others. If we are boxed in by quarreling, complacency, worry, blaming, and other acts of disobedience, we extinguish the light. But when we obey, we give a full measure of love, joy, sympathy, understanding, and compassion. Read samples from the Old Testament, such as stories from the book of Exodus, and see how God demands obedience, and how obedience sharpens our intake of light.

166

Spend much time studying, understanding, and applying verse 24. It is tremendous. Think deeply on what this parable is about. Yes, it is about the lamp, but what lights the lamp? (The Word.) How does the lamp reveal light? (When it is used.) How are we using the lamp to light the way for others?

If we receive only part of the Word, we receive very little. If we heed all that Jesus says, we receive wisdom, knowledge, and great understanding. Remember, it *is* possible for the light to be taken from us through carelessness, unbelief, or indifference. The more we put into hearing, the more we open up; thus, the more we receive. If we don't use what we get, we will lose all we get!

Prayer thought: We have faith enough when we in our helplessness turn to Jesus. (*Prayer*, p. 29)

LESSON 29

Mark 4:26-29, Growth of the Word

Here Jesus used an image of rural life in Palestine to talk about the kingdom of God. He compared God's kingdom to a man who scatters seed on the earth, patiently waits for it to grow, and joyfully reaps the harvest. Likewise, the disciples of Jesus would be scattering the Word. So they must learn to trust the seed to grow and relinquish the rest to God in faith and prayer. All his disciples need to do is plant the Word in people's hearts. The rest is done by the Word itself as it falls into the soil of human hearts—it's a daily miracle.

Jesus compared the seed in the ground to the growth in our lives, "First the stalk, then the head, then the full grain in the head." The roots are the hidden part of life, cultivated by faith and prayer. It's such a mystery! Will we ever learn that no human power causes the seed to sprout, and only divine power produces new life and the full grain—sanctification. What a beautiful parable showing that spiritual growing is a daily, continual process. To practice patience and humility in our lives and in church is difficult. We want to see the harvest, take credit for the stalk, the head, and the full head of grain, but God gives the increase. We plant! We sow the Word, which, when properly received, is full of life and power (Mark 4:1-9). So often, when no stalk or head seemed to appear, Merrill would say, "All we've been asked to do is diligently plant. God does the rest." Certainly God's Word will not return void (Isa. 55:10-11).

It's been interesting to note the *receptivity* of the Word, the *use* of the Word, and the *growth* of the Word. Did you know that Mark was so systematic and that he wrote in such an interesting way? What do you think his Gospel will show us about the Word in the following paragraph?

Prayer thought: Helplessness becomes prayer the moment that you go to Jesus and speak candidly and confidently with him about your needs. This is to believe. (*Prayer*, p. 30)

LESSON 30

Mark 4:30-32, Power of the Word

The tiny mustard seed is hardly bigger than a pinpoint, yet it is vital, alive, and full of vigor and heat. Certainly it amazed the disciples, who faced all the worldly opposition, to realize that God's kingdom could grow with such fantastic power. But the mustard seed is also a picture of the grace and power of the Word as it grows—the kingdom of God. "Since the mustard seed itself is the Kingdom, all who are in the Kingdom are part of the tree. The birds who rest in the branches are not members, only there temporarily."[11]

Don't miss this point: The power the Word possesses is yours for the asking. Jesus compared a little seed to the kingdom of God! What a teacher Jesus was! His purpose in this parable was to show the disciples the contrast between small beginnings and tremendous future growth. Christianity, with its small beginning, would increase to tremendous proportions. We can learn much from the way Jesus taught. He did not try to confuse people with intellectual data, but took the known and used it to illustrate the unknown. He wanted to challenge the true "growers" to study and mature by recalling his stories.

Prayer thought: It is not intended that our faith should help Jesus to fulfill our supplications. He does not need any help; all he needs is access. (*Prayer*, p. 30)

LESSON 31

Mark 4:33-34, Many Parables

Mark had the gift of saying what was necessary in just a few words. Can you see how these stories would fill the minds of hearers and be kindled into faith? Now, study again the beautiful order and progression of this unit. Notice the receptivity, use, growth, and power of the Word! One can never really finish studying this chapter!

Jesus spoke in parables not to confuse people, but to present pictures that would be long remembered. He spoke in parables to challenge those who sought to discover the true meaning and grow. Much of his teaching was against hypocrisy, but probably the false religious leaders would catch the vision too! What do you think?

We have completed Unit 5, Parables. See the outline on pages 10 and 11.

Prayer thought: Jesus cannot gain admittance until we "open the door," that is, until we in prayer give him an opportunity to intervene. (*Prayer*, p. 30)

LESSON 32

Mark 4:35-41, Power over Nature

This scene takes place on the Sea of Galilee, a charming bit of blue only twelve miles long and six miles wide, 680 feet below sea level. A long day of teaching over, Jesus was exhausted. He asked his disciples to turn the boat toward the solitude of the eastern shore to escape the crowds. The stern of the boat was a place for any distinguished stranger to relax on a carpet or cushion. Jesus, tired and worn out, needed rest, and relaxed perfectly in his Father's care. Soon, however, the boat was caught in a storm. Sudden storms on the Sea of Galilee were very common because the sea was surrounded by mountains and high hills that formed a deep trough for wild tempests.

Jesus rebuked the disciples' fear of the storm. After all, some of them were seasoned fishermen who had seen many storms. They seemed to imply that Jesus had to deliver them, as if they shouldn't have to face storms with him. When his overflowing grace came forth, they were full of awe—amazed by this mighty Servant who could handle the angry sea!

Prayer thought: Jesus has power also over my restless thoughts. He can rebuke the storm in my soul and still its raging water. (*Prayer*, p. 91)

LESSON 33

Mark 5:1-13, Power over Demons

The "other side of the sea" is the eastern side of the Sea of Galilee. The country of Gerasenes, which is located there, is a barren, desolate area. We learn much more about demons in this story. We can see their strength, their desire to abide in unclean places, their loneliness, and their dreadful awesomeness. We also see how impossible they are to control.

The question is often raised as to what is meant by demon possession. Some claim that it is merely a figurative expression for moral evil and depravity; others teach that it is descriptive of physical or more definitely of mental disease and specifically of insanity. No other narrative shows more clearly that demon possession denotes the mysterious but real control of a human body and soul by actual spirits of supernatural power—cruel, satanic, malign. It was not merely a disordered brain which enabled this poor sufferer at once to recognize Jesus as the "Son of the Most

High God"; it was not mental disease that feared to be sent "out of the country," that Jesus commanded to come out of the man and permitted to enter into the herd of swine. This man who met Jesus in "the country of the Gerasenes" was not a maniac but a demoniac.[12] Demons are evil or unclean spirits (Mark 1:23), and are fallen angels, servants of Satan (Matt. 12:26, 27). There is only one devil, but myriads of demons who serve the devil and make his power practically universal. A demoniac (Mark 5:1-20) is a person who personally has been invaded by one or more demons, who at will can speak and act through their human victim, deranging both his mind and body.[13]

Did Jesus ask the name to let the disciples know there were many demons? A Roman legion consisted of over six thousand men, so we know *legion* meant many! Matthew tells us they didn't want to be tormented before the time[14] (Matt. 8:29).

Notice the compassion of Jesus. He not only heard the loud cries of the demons, but also the agonizing call of the man. Imagine the disciples' amazement as the Master demonstrated his power over the demon world! "The unhindered power of God working through the sinless humanity of the Servant challenged the supernatural world and explains the outburst of demonism during his ministry."[15]

"Jesus is supreme master of the demon world whose will and word the demons must obey."[16]

We are living in an age of satanic warfare. How we need to commit our children and grandchildren to the Lord, asking the ministering angels to guard them each day.

Prayer thought: Unbelief is something very different from doubt. Unbelief . . . consists in people's refusal to believe . . . to see their own need, acknowledge their helplessness and go to Jesus and speak candidly and confidently. (*Prayer*, p. 30)

LESSON 34

Mark 5:14-20, The Departure

Gadara A.D. 31:

The people refused to receive Jesus' blessing. Notice the words *came*, *saw*, and *began to beg Jesus to leave*. This poem expresses so well the horror of rejecting Jesus.

Rabbi! begone! Thy powers
Bring loss to us and ours.
Our ways are not as Thine.
Thou lovest men, we swine.
Oh, get you hence, Omnipotence,
And take this fool of Thine!
His soul! What care we for his soul?
What good to us that thou has made him whole.
Since we have lost our swine.

And Christ went sadly.
He had wrought for them a sign
Of Love, and Hope and Tenderness divine.
They wanted swine.
Christ stands without your door and gently knocks
But if your gold, or swine, the entrance blocks
He forces no man's hold—He will depart.
And leave you to the treasures of your heart.

No cumbered chambers will the Master share,
But one swept bare
By cleansing fires, then plenished fresh and fair.
With meekness, and humility, and prayer.
There will he come, yet, coming even there
He stands and waits, and will no entrance win
Until the latch be lifted from within.[17]

Notice the people's values. They shunned the unclean, the untouchable, the poor, the lonely, but Jesus came as a Servant to restore and give new beginnings.

Decapolis (verse 20) refers to the region lying southeast of the Sea of Galilee, mainly Gentile territory. Jesus needed a living witness in this place as he reached out to the Gentiles. The man had to stay so that the people would do more than marvel. We will meet the results of this formerly possessed man later! What a changed Decapolis it will be!

Prayer thought: Doubt . . . is anguish, a pain, a weakness, which at times affects our faith. (*Prayer*, p. 30)

LESSON 35

Mark 5:21-24a, Jairus

Jesus returned to Capernaum the same day he met the demoniac. Jairus was one of the elders of the synagogue. This group was responsible to take care of the services and other affairs of the synagogue.

Note the ceaseless ministry of caring and love in this unit. Jesus identified with each individual at the point of that person's faith or lack thereof. Helplessness is so pronounced in this unit, and Jairus's faith was blessed as he openly confessed Jesus as his only hope.

Prayer thought: Doubt is faith-distress, faith-anguish, faith-suffering, faith-tribulation. It does serve to render us helpless. (*Prayer*, pp. 30-31)

LESSON 36

Mark 5:24b-34, Power over Sickness

This woman had had a flow of blood for twelve years. She had suffered much under physicians, had spent all of her money, and had grown worse, not better. Apparently, she heard reports about Jesus, and decided to exercise her faith. How the crowd must have pushed her back time after time! If they had known about her illness, they would have wanted to stone her. Only faith and courage enabled her to touch Jesus' garment.

Jesus gave her the great gift of physical, emotional, and spiritual health. Jesus wanted her to reveal herself, not for his sake, but for her own. Faith demands action! He pronounced her well publicly so she could go to her village and synagogue and be accepted in her home! The Jewish law could no longer isolate her.

Imagine what it was like for the disciples to see their Master demonstrate power over sickness!

Prayer thought: "To pray in the name of Jesus is . . . the deepest mystery in prayer." (*Prayer*, p. 56)

LESSON 37

Mark 5:35-43, Power over Death

Don't overlook the impact the woman's healing must have made on Jairus. What a conflict between faith and fear Jairus must have felt! I can almost see Jesus putting his hand on Jairus's shoulder and saying, "Do not fear, only believe." With every step Jairus took toward home, he must have thought, *Only believe, only believe—But death! Only believe, do not fear.*

Were Peter, James, and John chosen because they had come so much further spiritually than the other disciples? Perhaps. In the Old Testament, three witnesses were needed to verify the truth of an event (Deut. 17:6). Jesus gave strict commands because an outburst of excitement in response to such an amazing miracle might have hindered his work. Also, Jesus, in his tenderness, did not want the child to be terrified by a great mob!

When Jesus arrived, he found a house full of noise, sobbing, and wailing. In Palestine the deceased had to be buried on the same day they died, so the Jewish mourning began immediately.

The wailing women and the flute players were paid professionals, and we may be sure that for this prominent family and for the loss of an only child, they staged their best performance. With hair streaming wildly, beating their breasts violently, these women uttered loud, heart-rending wails and bursts of sobs. . . .Rising above their noise came the piercing sounds of the flutes. . . .[18]

Mark used the original Aramaic words to record what Jesus uttered. Then he translated them into Greek for his readers. Think of the parents' feelings of awe and terror. Jesus broke it. Notice the child got up, walked, and ate. What a wonder-working Servant he is! He even has power over death!

Jesus came to make all things new—even you. He loved people: the unclean, the untouchable, the mentally ill, the sick, the dying, the ones of low self-esteem, the rich, the ones burdened with grief, the lonely, the depressed, and the ones with no purpose in life. He gave them a new beginning.

We have completed Unit 6, Miracles. See the outline on pages 10 and 11.

Prayer thought: "I believe; help my unbelief" (Mark 9:24). We often condemn our doubt as unbelief but in Jesus' eyes, it is faith, if one is helpless and turns to him. (*Prayer*, p. 33)

LESSON 38

Mark 6:1-6a, Nazareth

Nazareth was eighteen miles from the Sea of Galilee. Why did Jesus return where he wasn't welcome? A real servant is long-suffering, and we know Jesus wanted to give the people of Nazareth a chance to hear the good news.

However, their unbelief limited Jesus' power and he could do no mighty work there.

Did you notice that Jesus was amazed? Jesus is twice recorded as having been amazed: once at a Gentile's faith (Luke 7:9), and once at his townspeople's unbelief. How tragic it is to hear the Word and not accept it. The people of Nazareth thought they knew Jesus, but because in their eyes he was only a carpenter, a common laborer, they refused to accept him. If they had truly known Jesus, wouldn't they have loved him? The tragedy is, these people admitted that Jesus had wisdom, did mighty works, and proclaimed a wonderful message, but they denied his claims. The Messiah, they thought, was not to come as a carpenter but as a king.

We learn here that Jesus had four brothers. His sisters had evidently married and lived around Nazareth. His earthly father, Joseph, had probably died, because he is not mentioned.

Prayer thought: We can begin by telling Jesus about our doubts and our weak faith. This makes it easier for us, and we can pray more confidently. (*Prayer*, p. 34)

LESSON 39

Mark 6:6b-13, Two by Two

Jesus responded to the opposition (6:1-6a) by sending out his disciples on their trial run. Their instructions were practical and clear. Jesus gave no long preparation and required no burdensome equipment.

Teamwork was necessary! Going two by two provided strength and encouragement to his disciples. Their power would increase as each gave his testimony. Jesus equipped them with his own power. His "orders" showed them that they were absolutely dependent on him. He was getting them ready for their worldwide mission.

The disciples were sent to proclaim the true message of repentance; they were not responsible for people who rejected it. If anyone refused to welcome them or refused to hear their message, it was a sign of rejection, an insult to their Master. The pious Jews often dusted their feet after journeying through Gentile territory. As a similar symbolic gesture, Jesus told his disciples to shake off the dust of any town that rejected them.

The practice of anointing with oil was a familiar remedy for healing. Oil was also a tangible reminder of the Holy Spirit and the spiritual healing that accompanies the joy of repentance and faith in Jesus. It is interesting that Mark mentioned anointing with oil here because he did not mention it again in his Gospel.

Ask Jesus to teach you what repentance entails. An old saint, a pastor, said on his deathbed, "Oh, if only I could preach again—repentance would be my theme."

Prayer thought: I need not be frightened away by my doubts, or my weak faith but only tell Jesus how weak my faith is, and I have let Jesus into my heart. He will fulfill my heart's desire. (*Prayer*, p. 34)

LESSON 40

Mark 6:14-16, Who Is Jesus? and Mark 6:17-29, Herod

Jesus' miracles and words plus the surprising acts of his disciples even reached the Herod's ears! This was Herod Antipas. He was only a tetrarch, so his power was somewhat limited. However, the royal title was given to him.

Each person faces the awesome responsibility of reporting who Jesus is, in life as well as in words. The people's reports made Jesus out to be a mere man.

Notice the two great forces at work here—love and hate! Notice how Herod repeatedly disobeyed his conscience. In contrast, look at the act of mercy by John's disciples. I'm sure they were full of fear and sorrow!

It is interesting that Mark included this gruesome story in his Gospel. Do you think he was suggesting that this is what the disciples of Jesus would face—opposition and death like John the Baptist?

Prayer thought: Jesus never grew tired of inviting, prompting, encouraging, exhorting, even commanding us to pray. (*Prayer*, p. 35)

LESSON 41

Mark 6:30-44, Feeding the Five Thousand

Now the multitudes have become excited about the disciples too. Try to imagine what it was like for Jesus to know the importance of having time alone with the disciples, but being so busy they had "no leisure even to eat."

Jesus seemed to have two reasons for wanting to be alone with the disciples. First, to talk about John's death, and, second, to share their experiences. How much they needed a quiet, undisturbed conference with their Master! Luke 9:10 mentions that they went to Bethsaida on the northern shore of the Sea of Galilee, at the lake entrance of the upper Jordan. Find it on the map on page 240. At this point on the shore, the people could easily cross by wading.

Carefully note the details of the feeding: Jesus' taking the inventory of food, having the people sit down in groups of one hundred and of fifty, blessing the loaves, giving them to the disciples to distribute, blessing the fish, and giving them to the disciples to distribute. The people ate until they were satisfied, and the disciples gathered up the leftovers.

As the day of teaching drew to a close, Jesus demonstrated the greatest reality of all—that he was the bread of life (John 6:35). All day long the people had eaten spiritually and satisfied the hunger of their souls. Feeding the crowd physically was not only an act of compassion, but also an act of creation. As Jesus broke the bread, he demonstrated that his body would be broken on the cross. How much that multitude needed his broken body!

Prayer thought: Jesus desires to answer our prayer, graciously and abundantly. (*Prayer*, p. 36)

LESSON 42

Mark 6:45-46, Time for Quiet, and
Mark 6:47-52, Walking on the Sea

Even the disciples would have loved to make Jesus king, but Jesus had to show them what kind of King he really was! As you study this lesson, don't forget that most of the disciples were experienced fishermen. The first watch was from 6:00 to 9:00, the second 9:00 to 12:00, the third 12:00 to 3:00, and the fourth 3:00 to 6:00. Some versions of the Bible note that Jesus' walking on the sea occurred during the fourth watch.

Jesus had fed the five thousand and had proven his power over nature, demons, disease, and death. Why were the disciples amazed by the way he handled the sea? Would they ever learn to accept the power of their Lord? Jesus purposely walked by the disciples because he wanted them to invite him into the boat. They needed to realize more and more that this Servant, their Master, *is* the Son of God Almighty. But the disciples' trouble was in their hearts. "In Greek the heart is believed to be the center of the mental and spiritual life."[19] What lessons Jesus was teaching them during their internship!

Prayer thought: A child of God can grieve Jesus in no worse way than to neglect prayer. (*Prayer*, p. 36)

LESSON 43

Mark 6:53-56, Gennesaret

Gennesaret is a small, triangular plain south of Capernaum on the northwest side of the Sea of Galilee. Does it surprise you that although the disciples were slow to believe in Jesus' power, the multitudes expected great things?

This paragraph closes the disciples' period of internship. They have learned that Jesus' kingdom is rejected by his home community, but welcomed in the small villages. They have also experienced the strength of supporting each other by going out two by two and practicing what they have been taught. They also have seen the two great forces of love and hate. But how little they knew of their King who fed five thousand and walked on the sea!

What tremendous power Mark packed into a few lines! This paragraph shows how people flocked to Jesus to take advantage of his healing powers and to hear his words. What a striking contrast the multitudes were to the religious leaders of the day. The Gospel of Mark is full of contrast.

We have now completed Unit 7, Internship. See the outline on pages 10 and 11.

Prayer thought: Many neglect prayer to such an extent that their spiritual life gradually dies out. (*Prayer*, p. 37)

LESSON 44

Mark 7:1-8, Unwashed Hands

This delegation from Jerusalem had traveled by foot sixty to seventy miles in order to spy on Jesus and expose him before the multitude. The people were divided into two camps—those who were for and those who were against Jesus. The popularity among the masses was growing, but so was the opposition from the religious leaders.

The bitter opposition to Jesus was fueled by tradition. Jesus and his disciples obeyed the levitical law, which was necessary in the Old Testament to keep the lineage pure. But religious leaders, who wanted to appear holy before the people instead of glorifying God, had added 613 laws to the levitical law. The washing of hands was one of the laws added by these leaders, and it had become a religious ceremony. Laws regulated the amount and kind of water to be used, who was to pour the water, and what kind of dish was to be used. For example, the water had to be poured over the hands as the hands were extended into the air in order that the water could run off the elbow. Thus they were assured of no defilement, which came from touching a Gentile, hog, dead body, or anything a Gentile had touched. It was a complicated system!

The disciples and Jesus did not eat with physically unclean hands, but merely abandoned the Jewish tradition of ceremonial washing. These traditions had become more important to the Jewish leaders than God's Word. Just as Isaiah had warned, the people honored God with their lips but had cold hearts: Their worship was wrong. In this intensive lesson, Jesus rebuked all unnecessary formalism in religion.

Prayer thought: Jesus has all that we need, and there is nothing that he would rather do than impart to us his gifts. (*Prayer*, p. 37)

LESSON 45

Mark 7:9-13, Corban

Watch what happens in this crucial lesson. Jesus never sidestepped the issue. He was always honest and fair—for the erring person's sake as well as for those he was teaching.

Exodus 20:12; 21:17 shows how seriously God demands respect for parents. The Fourth Commandment is the only commandment with a promise.

The Pharisees claimed that one could withhold support for a needy parent by declaring "corban" over any property. Such property would then be dedicated to God. "Corban," meaning gift, was simply a vow dedicating money to the temple. Often this property was used by the owners while their parents lived in want. If the Pharisees were refusing to help and love their parents and forgetting their vow, they were robbing the divine Word of its authority.

These religious leaders had become so involved in their traditions that their added laws had become more important than God's laws. They were spiritually blind. Jesus had to show his disciples the hypocrisy of the Pharisees' behavior. A new beginning required that his followers give up the luxury of being right.

Prayer thought: Do we go about at home and in the assembly of believers like spiritual cripples, starved and emaciated? (*Prayer*, p. 37)

LESSON 46

Mark 7:14-16, Listen, and Mark 7:17-23, Within and Without

What a revolutionary challenge Jesus presented. What a radical lesson! This message was so vital that Jesus began with the words, "Listen to me, all of you, and understand." He told his audience to shake off the old, fixed ideas and laws that obsessed the Pharisees. He reminded them that the heart is the center of an individual. His message was the opposite of the teachings of the Pharisees regarding defilement. They washed their hands ceremonially to be clean and stressed the cleanliness of body instead of spirit. Christ said that defilement comes from within, not from without. True defilement is that of the soul. It's not what we eat, but what we think and do that defiles us. Jesus wasn't as concerned about the stomach and intestines as he was about the heart, mind, will, and attitude.

Was Jesus preparing the way for the abolishment of the levitical law? Was it Jesus' radical attitude toward Jewish law that got him into trouble? Jesus here proclaimed that a person's nature is evil. Martin Luther in the *Small Catechism* says that all sins and evil lusts should be drowned by daily sorrow and repentance and be put to death, and that the new person should come forth daily and rise.[20] How difficult it is to face our sinful nature!

Prayer thought: We develop an unwilling spirit, which always finds pretexts for not praying and excuses for having neglected prayer. (*Prayer*, p. 39)

LESSON 47

Mark 7:24-30, Greek Woman

After exposing the hypocrisy and formalism of the proud Pharisees, Jesus went up north into Gentile territory. He deliberately left the populous centers of strife and bustle and headed for the quiet villages. He had more intensive training to give his disciples.

The "children" Jesus spoke of are Jewish. They came first as far as Jesus' mission on earth was concerned. The Jews were God's chosen people in the Old Testament. They had been given the Word and the great prophets. But there could always be scattered crumbs, or blessings, for the dogs, or Gentiles.

Notice the woman's faith. She didn't take offense at Jesus' statement about who was more important. How quickly she picked up on the thread of hope. She grasped the hidden truth in Jesus' clever answer. She would not be turned away, for she was willing to take just a crumb, like that a pet dog receives at his master's table. What a woman of wit, understanding, faith, and insight!

For the present time Jesus' work was for the Jews, but now the disciples had a glimpse of the great truth that salvation is for the Gentiles also. Here Jesus was laying the foundation for the future church. Here is the first hope for you and me. Notice, too, that Jesus' authority over demons was all powerful. It spanned space. He did not have to be present to cast the demon from the woman's daughter.

Prayer thought: To pray is difficult for us. It feels like too much of an effort. (*Prayer*, p. 38)

LESSON 48

Mark 7:31-37, Be Opened

The Decapolis was a region southeast of the Sea of Galilee. Jesus now was devoting his time to teaching his disciples in regions away from his enemies. He desired to help people he had not reached before. People in the Decapolis had heard the news of Jesus from the healed demoniac (Mark 5:1-20). Think how excited he must have been to tell Jesus about everything. What a living witness he was! The people who had before requested to leave the country now brought the sick to him.

Notice Mark's minute details and striking vividness as he recorded this event. Did you notice Jesus' extreme care and thoughtfulness? He had two senses to work with—sight and touch. Imagine yourself as this man—deaf and mute. Notice the steps Jesus took to heal him: took him aside (in quiet as the man was unaccustomed to sound), put fingers into his ears (the man couldn't hear), spat and touched his tongue (the man had a speech impediment), looked up to heaven (the place of divine help), sighed (yearning for God's help), and said, "Be opened." Did you catch Jesus' compassion and his communication in sign language?

Notice that Jesus also sought to arouse faith in the man. It's interesting to note that toward the end of his ministry Jesus seemed to stress the importance of faith in him.

Jesus "charged them to tell no one" as he did not want to be known as a miracle worker, but had a new message! True thankfulness is best expressed by obeying Christ even if we want to tell. There is such a fine line in witnessing. Is it seasoned with praise of self or praise of God?

What an eye opener for the disciples—what intensive training to see one region change so radically. Here they beheld what one man excited about Jesus could do!

Prayer Thought: Prayer is a fine, delicate instrument. To use it right is a great art, a holy art, the greatest art.

LESSON 49

Mark 8:1-10, Feeding the Four Thousand

"In those days" means that Jesus was teaching and healing in the region of the Decapolis, which was Gentile territory. The disciples seemed to have learned a little since the feeding of the five thousand. They were not telling Jesus what to do (Mark 6:35-36), but they did ask a doubting question. Notice Jesus' unfailing patience, love, and compassion throughout this paragraph. Remember, this was a period of intensive training for the Twelve because only a few months remain until Jesus dies on the cross.

Matthew 15:38 tells us there were four thousand men in the crowd, excluding the women and children. Let your mind dwell on this great miracle and its effect on those present. Jesus not only gave them physical bread but also nourishment for the soul. Notice, too, that the five thousand feeding (Mark 6) was in Jewish territory, and the four thousand feeding was in Gentile territory.

Dalmanutha lies on the western side of the lake. Matthew called it Magadan (Matt. 15:39).

Prayer thought: Prayer requires neither great native ability, nor much knowledge, nor money. The least gifted, the uneducated and the poor can cultivate the holy art of prayer. (*Prayer*, p. 40)

LESSON 50

Mark 8:11-13, Requests Sign

This paragraph is almost laughable! Jesus had crisscrossed the land with signs and miracles. He is the supreme sign, plainly demonstrating that he is the Messiah, the Son of God. Still, the Pharisees were ready to attack.

Although he was brief, Mark showed Jesus' deep emotions. Jesus sighed because of his grief at the hardness of the Pharisees' hearts. Where there is no faith, there is unbelief. The Pharisees demanded a sign from heaven like those recorded in Josh. 10:12-13 and 1 Sam. 7:9-10, but Jesus saw through the temptation and sailed away to the eastern side of the lake.

God's divine grace is always present and Jesus sincerely wanted to win the Pharisees as well as his disciples. But the Pharisees, in their hardness of heart, had decided they would not believe. What an important lesson this was for the disciples to learn!

A friend of mine came out of a court trial crushed and burdened. As she walked down the aisle alone, she whispered, "Oh, God, are you here? I need a miracle!" As she walked outside, snowflakes in all their beauty and glitter dazzled before her. In joy she whispered, "Thank you, Father." She received his grace!

Prayer Thought: Certain requirements also must be met if the art of prayer is to be acquired . . . practice and perseverance. (*Prayer*, p. 40)

LESSON 51

Mark 8:14-21, Yeast of the Pharisees

In the previous paragraph, Jesus left by boat for the other side of the lake, which was not populous. Jesus again sought lonely places to give his disciples more intensive training. On the western side, there would have been no concern about food! The disciples were still preoccupied with their lack of bread (one loaf was the size of a large biscuit) while Jesus was concerned with the basis of their faith.

Leaven or yeast is used here in reference to the corrupt teachings of the Pharisees and of Herod. Leaven was a symbol of evil such as hypocrisy, formalism, and materialism. Jesus was trying to help the disciples comprehend the false teachings they would be compelled to combat. They were to use their heart, eyes, ears, mind, reasoning powers, and will in order to understand his message. It was vital to use all the gifts God had given to preach the gospel.

Prayer thought: The Spirit of prayer can teach us to pray. Through the Word and daily exercise of prayer, he gives us the practice and the divine insight. (*Prayer*, p. 41)

LESSON 52

Mark 8:22-26, Restored Sight

This is Bethsaida-Julias on the eastern side of the lake near the entrance of the Jordan River. Jesus did not fulfill the people's request by merely touching the blind man, for he wanted to kindle faith within the man. Therefore, Jesus *took him* (to get away from the excitement of the city), *led him* (by the hand), *put saliva on his eyes* (touching him), *laid his hands on him* (symbolizing a great blessing to come), *asked* (got the man to realize his sight was being restored), *laid* (again, the touch), and *sent him home* (the deep impression of his experience with Jesus must be nurtured at home).

Jesus healed this man gradually because of his compassion and will. His power is immeasurable at any time, so he can always heal by touch, word, or will. But think of the beautiful act of touch—the blind man walking away from the multitude with his hand in Jesus' hand, the touch of Jesus' hands on his eyes. Jesus was preparing the man's faith to receive his love, compassion, and healing step by step. Our healing, too, is often very gradual. Jesus sent the man home because he needed to see and tell his loved ones first.

What a Servant Jesus is! This intensive lesson of love was a great lesson for his disciples. Are you taking time to gaze in awe at Jesus?

Prayer thought: To pray is to tell Jesus what we lack. Intercession is to tell Jesus what we see that others lack. (*Prayer*, pp. 44, 45)

LESSON 53

Mark 8:27-30, The Great Confession

Jesus next led his disciples to a more secluded country around Caesarea Philippi (pagan cities devoted to the worship of Baal). The group did not return to Capernaum until Jesus was ready to go to Jerusalem to take up the cross. He had deep, difficult lessons to teach his disciples. Would they be ready?

The disciples had seen Jesus' popularity and the opposition to his teachings. He had taught them in parables and miracles and had even sent them out on internship. After taking them through some intensive training, Jesus now asked them the all-important question—*who is He?* Think how the disciples must have discussed this among themselves! Peter, speaking for the group, passed the test; he confessed that Jesus *is* the divine Messiah, the Son of God, the long awaited Savior, the atoning Christ (John 1:40-41).

Knowledge of Jesus or just having been baptized long ago in the powerful name of the Trinity does not make anyone a disciple of Jesus. Becoming a disciple requires a daily growing, a daily understanding and commitment (Rom. 6:4).

Unit 8, Intensive Training, Mark 7:1—8:30, is now complete. Review what the disciples learned. See the master outline on pages 10 and 11.

Prayer thought: We learn to know Jesus so well that we feel safe when we have left our difficulties with him. (*Prayer*, p. 46)

LESSON 54

Mark 8:31-33, Jesus' Cross

In the previous paragraph we saw that the disciples had begun to comprehend the divine person of Jesus, but in this paragraph they began to see the Servant's greatest task—his passion, his work of redemption. Jesus had spoken of his death in veiled terms, but now he began to speak of it openly, breaking the terrible news to his dearest friends. This was the first open announcement of his forthcoming death. How could they begin to understand the meaning of his death if they didn't know who he was?

Jesus said he must (1) suffer many things (there is still a veil over the details); (2) be rejected by the elders (they were older, experienced men of the Jewish nation who acted as judges in the local courts); (3) be rejected by the chief priests (that is, members of the high priests, Caiaphas's family); (4) be rejected by the scribes (writers and interpreters of the religious and ceremonial laws), and (5) be killed in Jerusalem (Luke 13:33). Jesus told the disciples he would rise again, but they seemed so concerned about his being killed that they never grasped the significance of the last promise. Jesus would arise not in the future but three days after his death—what joy!

Seventy-one men served on the Sanhedrin, the highest judicial and religious court of the Jewish nation. The disciples knew that the Sanhedrin had planned to destroy Jesus, but thus far Jesus had frustrated their plans. At this time Jesus told the disciples that the Sanhedrin would succeed. No, he didn't dare tell them by what means he would be killed. That he would make known later. To see their Master a victim of the Sanhedrin must have overwhelmed his followers. Remember the name of this unit, Crisis Week.

Yes, Peter criticized Jesus when he spoke about what was to come. Peter was ready to follow a popular Messiah, but not a suffering one. Jesus' rebuke did not imply that Peter was satanic, but that by urging Jesus to sidestep the cross, he was taking the side of the tempter. Remember, the cross is an offense to many people. Did the disciples really understand the meaning of the Messiah? Jesus would not be an earthly Christ, as the disciples had hoped. He would be a suffering Messiah, for suffering was necessary to usher in God's kingdom.

Prayer thought: Leave entirely to God the "when and how" concerning the fulfillment of our prayer to God. (*Prayer*, p. 50)

LESSON 55

Mark 8:34—9:1, The Disciples' Cross

What is a cross? We should probably start by asking, "What misconceptions do we have of a cross today?" When we see a child who has a handicap we may say, "What a cross!" No, that isn't a cross, necessarily. When an accident befalls someone, we may say, "Isn't that a hard cross?" Not necessarily. When someone dies in a family, we may say, "What a cross!" No, again.

Listen. *A cross is not doing what I want to do, but what God wants me to do.* Someone tells me some juicy gossip and I call my best friend to repeat the news. If I hear the voice of God saying, "That's sin; don't tell," I have the option of taking up the cross. If I tell, I've gone the way of the flesh and denied the cross. If I listen to his voice and talk about something else, I've done God's will and have taken up the cross. When God's will crosses our will, and we choose to follow his will, this is taking up the cross.

Taking up the cross means to die to self. It involves the denial of self-praise, self-importance, self-glory—you name it—the denial and death of self. Self-denial simply entails giving up food, drink, or pleasure for a season. Denial of self, however, means giving our body, soul, and mind to Jesus—dying to self. Is your cross an illness, loneliness, lost job, big ego, divorce, or low self-esteem? You see, loneliness can become a cross when it becomes self-pity. We must make the decision to give it up and let Christ take it!

The closer we live to Christ, the more crosses we will bear. As we grow closer to Christ, his will becomes more and more our will. The unconverted may have many sorrows, but no crosses. A cross is something we take up because we are Christians. Only the Holy Spirit can reveal to us the magnitude of Jesus' cross, our cross.

Our will is the issue (Mark 3:35). Jesus doesn't pull his sheep by a rope. In his army we are volunteers. His grace draws our will and wins it for himself. His grace includes everyone. Don't forget that by losing our life for his sake and the gospel's, we find it.

Notice Mark 8:38. This is the awful punishment to those who are ashamed of Christ and do not carry the cross. Now look at Mark 9:1.

The Jews saw the kingdom of God come with power. They saw it at the crucifixion, ascension, and Pentecost, and as thousands turned to Christ. In this verse Mark perhaps referred to the destruction of Jerusalem, which took place in the years 66 to 70 A.D., when ninety thousand Jews were sold into slavery and the official Jewish nation was abolished.

Prayer thought: When the Spirit has taught us that ... he decides when and how our prayers are to be answered, then we will experience rest and peace when we pray. (*Prayer*, p. 52)

LESSON 56

Mark 9:2-8, The Great Confirmation of the Cross

What an experience for the three disciples! Remember, three witnesses were necessary for proof in Old Testament history, and these three seemed to be Jesus' inner circle. Moses represents the law; Elijah, the prophets; and Christ, the fulfillment of both.

Instinctively and spontaneously, Peter drew upon one of the greatest experiences of joy his people enjoyed, the annual communal celebration of the Feast of Booths, the Feast of Tabernacles. At the Feast of Tabernacles, booths or shelters were erected. Booths were temporary quarters used for seven days in commemoration of the days in Egypt. It was the most joyous of feasts (Deut. 16:13-16).

> Each year the Jewish people looked forward to this great festival. After the autumn harvest, they came in one great pilgrimage to the sanctuary to offer praise and thanksgiving for God's abundant goodness to them and to ask the Lord to send rains for the coming year. To accommodate the many people, small booths or tents were constructed wherever there was space, on hillsides and housetops and in the corners of courtyards. The booths were made of palm branches and decorated with fruit. There was little time for sleeping during the joyous, week-long festival. The entire time was merriment and praise. The memories of the splendor of this great feast sustained and nurtured the Jewish people throughout the entire year.[21]

We heard the Father's statement at Jesus' baptism too. The Father was confirming what Peter confessed in Mark 8:29. Jesus was facing the cross and needed his Father's confirmation. Don't you think the Father's confirmation helped prepare Jesus for the mental pain and death he was facing? How can we begin to grasp how Jesus endured the cross? We treat the cross so casually—wear it, display it, ignore it. Yet, the cross is the differential of the Christian religion, the power which enables the Christian to transcend the world and to win the victory.[22]

> [Human beings], though still in the flesh, were given a magnificent glimpse of the age to come, the unspeakable joy literally of looking into heaven. This leap from the sin of this world to the holiness of the next is breathtaking to contemplate (Rom. 12:2). . . . The Christian must make a break with the past so radical that his mind is filled with the thoughts of Christ himself. A faith which does not do this, which stops with the belief that being "saved" is the whole Christian experience, is dead and denies Christ's concern for all mankind.[23]

Prayer thought: We forget to pray in the name of Jesus. (*Prayer*, p. 54)

LESSON 57

Mark 9:9-13, The Great Prophet

Jesus was now fully ready to take the way to Jerusalem—the way of the cross. Visualize the great significance this transfiguration meant to the three disciples. After Christ's death, Peter told what he had seen in 2 Pet. 1:16-18, and John in John 1:14. Jesus here made clear the promise of Mal. 4:5-6, identifying John the Baptist as the Elijah to come before him. John "restored all things" by turning the nation in repentance back to God, and announcing the Lamb of God, the Messiah! How the three disciples must have wanted to tell everything then!

The disciples couldn't grasp the idea of Jesus' rising from the dead since he was very much alive. Even the disciples expected the Messiah to be an earthly king like David who would destroy their enemy, Rome. Their value system was not eternal but earthly!

"The Son of Man . . . is to go through many sufferings and be treated with contempt" (Mark 9:12). Jesus was trying to open the eyes of his followers to the awfulness of the cross. Yes, Jesus was the greatest prophet, but that is not sufficient. He came to be my Savior and Redeemer!

Prayer thought: The Spirit of prayer says, "Come in the name of Jesus. That name gives unholy humans access to a holy God." (*Prayer*, p. 56)

LESSON 58

Mark 9:14-29, The Great Failure

When I envision this scene, I see the crowd of curious people, the delighted scribes and Pharisees, the brave and anxious father, the helpless son, and the nine defeated disciples. How majestically Mark portrayed Jesus! He came into this stressful situation and stood in divine power and dignity, identifying with the suffering man and his son. What a mighty Servant!

Jesus allowed the father to confess his thoughts and feelings and then challenged him with the phrase "*if you are able.*" What a setback this man's faith must have suffered when the disciples failed to heal his son. Jesus wanted to show this man that his faith was not unbelief, but doubt. Hallesby says that unbelief is an attribute of the will and consists in people's refusal to believe . . . to see their own need, acknowledge their helplessness, go to Jesus . . . and speak candidly and confidently. Doubt, on the other hand, is anguish, a pain, a weakness, which at times affects our faith. We could therefore call it faith-distress, faith-anguish, faith-suffering, faith-tribulation.[24] Remember, to believe is a gift from God. We must ask for it!

It's so easy to talk about prayer and to discuss it, but the most important part of prayer is to pray! Difficult problems can be overcome only by prayer! Hallesby says Satan doesn't care how much we study or how much we work, just so we don't pray! How we need to fight Satan in order to spend time with Christ in prayer.

It is distressing to hear how many Christians say they are so busy that they spend little time if any in private prayer. On the other hand, we can rejoice about all the small prayer groups throughout the land. Power! Remember, Jesus didn't say we have to be in the hundreds. He said where "two or three are gathered" (Matt. 18:20). Try it! Remember to pray each day that all our churches will become havens of prayer, and that people will be invited quietly to bring their hurts, frustrations, differences, and joys as they sit in the pew or quietly go to the altar. May the body of Christ, the church, become sensitive to the hurts of all its members.

We have now completed Unit 9, Crisis Week (see pages 10 and 11). Only the Holy Spirit can help us grasp this unit.

Prayer thought: As we learn to pray in the name of Jesus, our hearts are so full of love that we would gladly carry the whole world to God in prayer. (*Prayer*, p. 55)

LESSON 59

Mark 9:30-32, The Second Announcement

Keep in mind that Jesus had withdrawn into Tyre and Sidon to teach his disciples deep truths. They had left Caesarea Philippi, twenty-five miles north of Capernaum, to journey through Galilee for the last time. This would be Jesus' last trip to Capernaum, his home.

Jesus sought the least traveled roads, as he needed this time to teach his disciples about the coming events—especially the cross. They had to realize that the cross was not a trap or incident in his career; it had always been the Savior's plan to give his life as a ransom for many. This was not a gloomy prediction, for each time he gave the glorious declaration, he promised that he would rise again! Don't you think Jesus used this journey for hours of meditation and prayer?

In this second announcement of his upcoming death, Jesus added just one more insight—he will be betrayed, a hint of Judas's treacherous act. Imagine what it must have been like for the disciples to realize that someone would be a traitor and give Jesus over to his enemies.

194

Jesus had always been so kind to explain their questions, but the disciples appear to have been too afraid to ask. How it would have helped them in the days ahead if they had only expressed their fear.

If you and I study Christ's cross, we, too, will be better prepared for our trials and temptations and become the persons God intended us to be.

Prayer thought: If we fail to [pray in the name of Jesus] our prayer life will either die from discouragement and despair or become simply a duty. (*Prayer*, p. 57)

LESSON 60

Mark 9:33-37, Who Is the Greatest?

This was probably the last time Jesus entered his earthly home. According to Jesus' question, the disciples had been behind him, in discussion. Notice that Jesus pressed on toward Jerusalem—the disciples toward greatness. The disciples were full of personal ambition, Jesus full of service. Jesus' idea was utter forgetfulness of self in constant service to others. Jesus "came not to be served but to serve" (Mark 10:45).

Jesus wanted to settle the question of greatness once and for all, so he used a parable. A child is helpless, frank, honest, and open and has the seeds of perfect faith. People who want to be great in the eyes of the world play up to those who have power to give advancement, but playing up to a child is hopeless, for a child can't promote the ambitions of those seeking greatness.

True greatness is a gift from God. Only as we keep our eyes on Jesus can we desensitize ourselves from the praise of the world and willingly stoop down to the humble place. Too often our ego raises its ugly head. Jesus never talked about the famous, but pointed to the faithful! How rich this principle of greatness has become in the true Christian church. Only as we keep our eyes on Jesus can we begin to live it! As we receive in Jesus' name, we receive him, and receive the Father. Powerful! (John 14:23)

Prayer thought: "Let anyone who is thirsty come to me, and let the one who believes in me drink." (John 7:37-38a)

LESSON 61

Mark 9:38-41, For or Against

In the previous paragraph, "Who Is the Greatest?" John may have begun to question what he and the other disciples had done. Here, Jesus gave his disciples a marvelous discourse on the blessedness of all work rendered in his name. The man the disciples criticized had cast out demons in Jesus' name. Do you admire John for his honesty and sensitive spirit, or was he exposing the jealousy of the Twelve?

Jesus answered John beautifully. He explained that if the man was really casting out demons and did so in Jesus' name, then he was using the right power! How Jesus encouraged John to be tolerant!

Did you notice the beautiful comparison: Casting out demons is powerful, but one can do a seemingly less significant act, such as giving a cup of cold water in Jesus' name, and that is powerful too. Doing good to others because of sympathy, guilt, or importance is human. However, doing good because of our love for Christ is truly Christian; it is being a servant. The name *Jesus* has power in the little situations and mundane daily tasks as well as in the big problems.

"Follow Christ, not the things people do in his name. Human beings will always let you down, Jesus never does."[25]

Prayer thought: Jesus waits only for one thing . . . that is for us to ask him to help us. (*Prayer*, p. 59)

LESSON 62

Mark 9:42-48, Millstone, and
Mark 9:49-50, Salt

A millstone is a large stone for grinding grain in a mill. What chance would even good swimmers have with millstones around their necks? We might squelch someone's faith by our set ideas. We might put millstones about people's necks because we love the luxury of being right. Do we criticize or encourage? Do we listen? We need to be sensitive to people's trials and love them. That is what God is like. "A bruised reed he will not break, and a dimly burning wick he will not quench" (Isa. 42:3).

Through three hyperboles, Jesus showed the enormity of the crime of misleading others. That sin, whatever it is, must be given up if it causes one to hurt another and to be unfaithful to Christ. Emotionally and spiritually, the sacrifice of giving up a favorite sin might hurt as much as the three examples Jesus gave (losing a hand, foot, or eye). Mutilating the body would not take care of the passions and lust in our hearts. It's the heart that must be changed.

Salt preserves, gives taste, and causes thirst. That's what the sanctifying Word does! Because of our Christ-centered life, are people around us thirsty for the Word?

Prayer thought: Hear me, not for my sake, nor for the sake of my prayer . . . but hear me for Jesus' sake (*Prayer*, p. 58)

LESSON 63

Mark 10:1, Judea, and Mark 10:2-9, Divorce

Don't forget the name of this unit. Jesus is still on the journey to Jerusalem. He has left Capernaum for the last time! "Beyond the Jordan" means east of the Jordan through Perea. Mark 10:1 is just a short paragraph, but close your eyes and use your imagination. Did Jesus say goodbye to anyone? Did his family know about the cross?

There were two Jewish schools of thought related to divorce. The school of Shammai said a man could not release his wife except for something indecent; the school of Hillel allowed bad cooking, no favor in a man's eyes, and other similar faults as an acceptable reason for divorce. Since Shammai was strict and Hillel was lax, the Pharisees put Jesus to the test.

Study how wisely Jesus handled the test. Jesus didn't agree with either side, but delivered a rebuke for "your hardness of heart." He referred them to their idol, Moses, and his teaching on divorce.

Notice the beauty of verse six. In Jesus' day, women were sometimes treated as property. Jesus corrected this policy and demanded oneness!

How divorced couples are hurting today! Life has become so deceitful, stressful, and complicated. There is no place where love and listening need to be practiced as much as among divided families, especially where children are involved. When one person of the body of Christ hurts, we all hurt. The Lord seeks to restore broken homes and heal damaged families. Jesus hates all sin, divorce included, because of the harm it causes in every life it touches. But his redemption covers all our sins, and the gospel gives us a new beginning.

Prayer thought: Jesus will not and cannot force himself into our distress. We must open ourselves to him. (*Prayer*, p. 59)

LESSON 64

Mark 10:10-12, Marriage, and
Mark 10:13-16, Children

We must never forget that marriage is a sacred and holy part of God's great plan. In the eyes of God, the rite of marriage is a one-time experience. Matthew declared unchastity as a basis for divorce. In Corinthians, divorce may occur if an unbelieving spouse leaves or separates.

Isn't this beautiful? Jesus had spoken about the sacredness of marriage, which makes a home secure. He next turned to the blessedness of children who complete and strengthen that tie.

A child in Jesus' time deserved nothing. How beautiful the love and generosity of these parents were. They cared and brought their children to Jesus so they would receive his memorable benediction!

Children are blessed with the gift of trust, helplessness, honesty, and faith. So Jesus pronounced a blessing on the children and reminded his listeners that the kingdom of God belongs to children (verses 14-15).

How often do you give your child a look of love or a touch? How often do you put your hand on a child in benediction? A child is such a gift from the Lord! Let us remember how much children need to be surrounded by blessing (verse 16). May we not allow our business and stress to drive them away.

Prayer thought: Jesus, the Lord of this power, will direct the necessary power to the desired place at once. (*Prayer*, p. 63)

LESSON 65

Mark 10:17-22, Rich Young Man

What a clever writer Mark was! This paragraph illustrates exactly the opposite kind of faith as the previous paragraph: not childlike faith, but faith in self and earthly possessions. But don't be too hard on this self-righteous inquirer. He was searching and honest, and he did something about his longings—he came to Jesus!

The man's emphasis, however, is "I." We think of him as a young man who had a good opinion of himself. Jesus challenged him on his thoughtless use of the word *good*. The man must have had riches and power, but Jesus was not threatened by the man's position and sought simply to convict him of his sin.

Jesus cleverly gave the rich man the test of the commandments, for the man really believed that he had kept the commandments. Even in the face of Jesus' questioning, the man didn't fall from his pedestal. Hence, Jesus probed further and showed him his real selfishness. The supreme test came when Jesus gave him five things to do: go, sell, give, come, and follow. The test showed that the man had broken Jesus' second commandment (Mark 12:31)—love for his neighbor.

Prayer thought: This weapon [of prayer] is the more valuable to the friends of Jesus, because it is not possible for the enemies of Jesus to make use of it. (*Prayer*, p. 63)

LESSON 66

Mark 10:23-27, Kingdom of God, and
Mark 10:28-31, Hundredfold

The previous paragraph and this one deal with riches, a great obstacle to salvation. Both of them reveal riches as a hindrance to entering heaven.

By looking around at his disciples, Jesus showed that he wanted to impress each one with what he was about to say. We must remember that in these days, wealth provided people with assurance of God's favor. So giving up riches wasn't an easy thing to do. However, the love of something, not merely possessing it, presents the problem. Possessing riches isn't necessarily a sin, but trusting in riches to enter the kingdom of God is wrong. Riches can be a great blessing if used correctly.

Jesus explained that we must become like a little child in order to enter the kingdom of God—stripped of all self-trust, self-righteousness, and greed. We must be willing to carry the cross and sacrifice anything that stands between us and Jesus Christ. Through his grace, God will give the ability to do so, for all things are possible with him. "All men have a secret longing for riches of some kind. The question is thus an implied confession on the part of the disciples. But another thing is not so excellent, namely, the confession that the disciples believed a man can and should do something on his part toward being saved."[26] The more we rely on Jesus, the more God's grace abounds. The kingdom of God is not a merited reward.

Notice the plurals in verse 30. Some may be rejected by their loved ones, but they will find blessed communion in the family of God. Sometimes persecutions of various sorts may be necessary to give us balance, depth, and joy (James 1:2)!

The prestige associated with riches, popularity, and earthly power might put a person in first place in this world, but he or she may be the last to accept Christ.

Prayer thought: Jesus extended his almighty arm so far down that we insignificant and sinful humans can reach it every time we bend our knees in prayer. (*Prayer*, p. 63)

LESSON 67

Mark 10:32-34, The Third Announcement

Can you imagine the disciples' stress, tension, and fear as Jesus pressed on toward Jerusalem ahead of them? Was it Jesus' facial expression, his attitude, or his majestic, unfaltering step that inspired their concern (Luke 9:51)?

Again, Jesus tried to prepare the disciples. He warned them about the horror of the crucifixion that would await him in Jerusalem. This time he mentioned he would be handed over to Gentiles, the Romans. This meant he would be condemned to death by crucifixion. Imagine the humiliation! But don't forget, he promised to arise after three days!

Compare the three announcements of Jesus' death that Mark recorded:

First-Mark 8:31	Second-Mark 9:31	Third-Mark 10:33
Son of Man	Son of Man	Son of Man
suffer	betrayed into human hands	Jerusalem handed over to chief priests and scribes
rejected by elders, chief priests, and scribes		condemn hand him over to the Gentiles
		mock
		spit flog
killed	will kill him	kill him
rise	rise	rise

Jesus' death and resurrection were no accident. It was a goal that Jesus had set before himself. God had planned it and it was progressing according to schedule.

Prayer thought: Whenever we touch his almighty arm, some of his omnipotence streams . . . out to others. (*Prayer*, p. 63)

LESSON 68

Mark 10:35-40, James and John, and
Mark 10:41-45, Not to Be Served, but to Serve

Mark spoke only about James's and John's desire for greatness, but from Matthew we learn that their mother desired it for them too! How stupid, inconsiderate, selfish, and blind their request seems to us. Jesus had just been speaking of being mocked, scourged, spit on, and crucified, but the brothers were still thinking of an earthly kingdom! Yet there is something beautiful in their request too. It is an expression of their faith in the kingdom of God.

What patience and love Jesus manifested in his response. The two disciples' request and answer to Jesus' question revealed pride and ignorance, but Jesus gently led them further in the faith. Jesus knows what is best for us! We are free to ask him anything, but we may be denied. These disciples had to begin to see the great lesson Jesus opened up to them in Mark 8:34—the way of the cross. James and John said they were willing to take the cup. In Acts 12:2 we see that James died as a martyr, and in Rev. 1:9 we learn that John lived in exile.

Which sin is worse—pride or jealousy? Even on this last journey to Jerusalem, the disciples were fighting and thinking of themselves! Yet Jesus patiently explained the law of true greatness once again (Mark 9:35). Instead of a rebuke, he lovingly used the opportunity to teach. Being a servant is the law of greatness in his kingdom. Jesus was showing the disciples he was not exempt from that law, for he was pressing on to the cross. "The way to the great places in the Kingdom lies only along the path of suffering."[27] To sum things up, Mark gave us that tremendous key verse—Jesus came to serve and to give (10:45)!

It's interesting to notice that the three announcements of Jesus' death are followed by expressions of personal ambition: a tool of the devil (8:32-33), greatness (9:33-37), and importance (10:35-45).

Luther says that Jesus treated the presumptuous pride of the Pharisees with severity, but the ambition of these disciples he treats with gentleness, for it springs from faith and needs only to be purified. Augustine said, "They sought the exaltation, but did not see the step."[28]

Prayer thought: Why doesn't Jesus grant our request? His love . . . is so great that he not only desires to give us what we ask for, but much more. (*Prayer*, p. 104)

LESSON 69

Mark 10:46-52, Blind Bartimaeus

Try to picture this scene: Jesus and his disciples on their way to Jerusalem; the blind Bartimaeus shouting to Jesus; the excited multitude, some of whom tried to hinder the blind beggar, while others tried to help him! The multitude was so huge that the blind man had to cry out for Jesus' attention.

Why did Mark only record this one healing on Jesus' journey to Jerusalem? Did you notice what Bartimaeus called Jesus? Yes! The Son of David! Does that mean anything to you? Yes, it is the true title for the Messiah. Bartimaeus was permitted to call it out twice. Do you see the revelation? Now that Jesus was going to Jerusalem, to his death, he was willing to openly accept the true messianic title. Heretofore he had avoided this title because his time had not yet come (Mark 1:34; 3:12). Now it was time for all to know that the Servant, this Jesus of Nazareth, was David's Son—true Messiah who would go willingly to his death for them.

What if blind Bartimaeus had obeyed the crowd and kept still? God could have found someone else to announce the Messiah, but God let nothing hinder Bartimaeus from reaching the Messiah. Bartimaeus helped prepare the people for Palm Sunday. We have seen Jesus as Prophet; now Bartimaeus introduced him as King. In a few days we shall see him as the true High Priest.

We have now finished Unit 10, Journey to Jerusalem. Review Jesus' days of teaching as he journeys. See the outline on pages 10 and 11.

Prayer Thought: The power of Jesus is entirely independent of time and space. In the very moment that we bend our knees and pray for all in foreign lands, in that same instant this power is transmitted to these people. (*Prayer*, p. 63)

LESSON 70

Mark 11:1-10, Triumphant Entry

Bethpage and Bethany were two little villages only a stone's throw apart and two miles from Jerusalem. They were near the Mount of Olives. One can still visit Bethany, but Bethpage no longer exists.

This is Sunday, Palm Sunday, and Mark 11:1-10 shows how popular Jesus had become. Envision the dramatic picture: Jesus was met by a host of excited people from Jerusalem. What fanfare! He came in as a king! Blind Bartimaeus had opened the way, and the hour had come for Jesus to openly say, "I am the promised One, the King of Israel."

Thus Jesus swept into Jerusalem as the royal Son of God, but notice that he sat on a donkey's colt—not on a horse like a glamorous king. Spreading their garments and leafy branches on the road the multitudes sang and quoted Scripture in homage to him (Ps. 118:26). First they proclaimed Jesus as King: "Hosanna." Then they offered a prayer: "*Blessed is the one who comes in the name of the Lord.*" Then they confessed that Jesus was truly from God: "*Blessed is the coming kingdom of our ancestor David.*" What a joyous confession they offered. No doubt Bartimaeus was there with his "seeing eyes," thankful to Jesus and joining in the praise.

Prayer thought: Our lives should be ... quiet but steadily flowing streams of blessing, which through our prayers and intercessions should reach our whole environment. (*Prayer*, p. 64)

LESSON 71

Mark 11:11, Temple Inspection, and
Mark 11:12-14, Fig Tree

The temple inspection was the first day of the week. Jesus walked about the temple, viewing the abuses that had again crept in. Afterward, he went to Bethany for safety because the authorities were anxious to arrest him and his time would not come until the eve of the Passover. He came to be the Passover Lamb and was in complete control of his destiny. We do not know with whom he stayed. Perhaps he stayed with Martha, Mary, and Lazarus or with Simon the Leper.

In the story of the fig tree, Mark revealed a miracle and parable— what a stroke of genius! This was Monday of Jesus' last week. Jesus may have risen early to go into the hills to pray, to talk to the Father. All we know is that he was hungry. Jesus could expect figs on the tree because some fig trees put out fruit and leaves simultaneously.

Jesus had healed and blessed. Here he used his divine power to destroy. His response was unusual, but Jesus had a divine lesson to portray. The fig tree was a prophecy of the judgment coming to the people. Think of all God had done for them and how they continued to reject him by their fruitlessness, pride, rebellion, hypocrisy, and scheming.

But here was this tree with all its grand display of foliage, all nothing but empty pretense, and where it led one to expect that it might have at least a few figs already fit to eat, it had absolutely nothing at all, "nothing but leaves."[29]

Prayer thought: We should say to God as we mingle with our dear ones each day, "God, give them each your blessing. They need it, because they live with me." (*Prayer*, p. 64)

LESSON 72

Mark 11:15-19, Cleansing of the Temple

This was Monday of the last week. Cattle and doves were necessary for the temple sacrifices and abounded everywhere. The animals brought were often exchanged for more perfect ones, thus, the buying and selling. A tax also had to be collected, only in Jewish coins, from every Israelite twenty years of age or older. Thus, foreign coins had to be exchanged. The outer court of the temple, the Gentile court, was desecrated with this lucrative monopoly that the temple authorities operated to a profitable advantage. Herod had built this outer court so that his Gentile subjects (Egyptians, Greeks, or Romans) could go in a part of the temple. During the Passover the outer court was full of tables, stalls, and bartering! Notice the authority in the five verbs Mark used to describe Jesus' actions—*entered, drive, overturned, would not allow,* and *was teaching.*

The temple had been carefully arranged so that everything within it caused a person to turn to God. The Sanhedrin, the chief priests and scribes, were in charge here, but Jesus challenged their actions and called them to repentance. By his authority he claimed that he was the Messiah. On Palm Sunday, he presented himself as their Savior and King. Here he declared himself Lord of the temple. What a bombshell!

Prayer thought: God is not only good; he is also omniscient, knowing at all times what is best for us. It is not necessary for us to try to teach him what is best for us by argumentation, persuasion, or much talking. (*Prayer*, p. 102)

LESSON 73

Mark 11:20-24, Fig Tree Withered, and
Mark 11:25-26, Forgive

This was Tuesday of the last week, and Jesus was returning to Jerusalem. Peter seemed surprised when he saw the shriveled fig tree and said, "It really happened! It's withered!" Jesus replied, in effect, "If you have faith in God you can do this too, Peter."

Jesus made it clear that the power of God was at work (John 14:12; 15:4-5). He explained to Peter that he must do two things: ask, or put his request into words, and believe that he would receive; and relinquish his request to the Father. Jesus further explained that Peter must not pray with an unforgiving heart. There must be nothing between a believer and God.

How easily we toss the word *faith* around. Hallesby says that if you even think of bringing your prayer to Jesus, you've got enough faith to start! I'm so happy in this century we realize the great importance of little groups for Bible study and discussion—just two, or three, or six people! Have you discovered the joy of praying in sentence prayers with each other, back and forth? It's always easiest to start with thanksgiving! What is most important about prayer? No theologian or intellectual can argue with me. The most important thing is doing it! Not that we will pray, not that we hope to later, not that we plan to, but that we actually take time to do so. Prayer levels mountains!

A pastor from Papua New Guinea was amazed at some of our churches in America. He said that in his country if one member of the body of Christ hurts, the whole body of Christ hurts. In America are we often too busy, too preoccupied, or too cold to listen?

Prayer thought: "You do not have, because you do not ask." (James 4:2b)

LESSON 74

Mark 11:27-33, First Clash

Now the clashes in the temple begin. It's Tuesday morning of the last week. Keep in mind that those who attack Jesus are the high priests, scribes, and elders. They compose the Sanhedrin, which functions as the supreme court of the Jews.

"These things" that the Sanhedrin asked Jesus about refer to his royal entry into Jerusalem, his cleansing of the temple, his claim that the temple was his house, his miracles, and his powerful authority. The first clash occurred because Jesus threatened their authority. If Jesus said his authority was from God, they would have pronounced him a blasphemer. If he claimed his own authority, they would have named him a fanatic. Instead of falling into their trap, Jesus asked them a question and demanded an answer.

Jesus' response implied that John's authority was divine as was his, but the Sanhedrin sidestepped the issues. The high court was forced to say, "We do not know." Jesus knew they knew, the people knew they knew, but they weren't honest. Jesus had discredited his enemies before the people!

First Clash:

Who	Question	Jesus' Answer	Effect
Chief priests, scribes, and elders	By what authority?	Asked a question	Silenced, disgraced

Prayer thought: If you have a pain deep down in the most sensitive region of your soul, your conscience, then point it out to Jesus. (*Prayer*, p. 96)

LESSON 75

Mark 12:1-11, Vineyard

The Sanhedrin seemed to have planned to leave, but Jesus had other plans. In the first clash they refused to answer Jesus' question so he refused to answer theirs. But now he answered their question in a parable.

Jesus spoke with bold realism, no mincing of words. God's patience toward Israel had been one of mercy, mercy, and more mercy. The wine growers of the parable (Israel) stood before him and he looked them squarely in the eye as he exposed their hypocrisy and devilish acts. They were murderers! God had brought Israel from Egypt to Canaan. He had planted them, fenced them in, equipped them, and given them community and ceremonial laws—everything they needed. The tenants were the people (Israel) to whom God had given the vineyard; the servants were the prophets, including John the Baptist; and the son was Jesus. This parable gives us such a marvelous lesson on Jesus' claims of divine authority and how he bravely went to the cross. It exposes Jesus' coming death, but also his victory. What a warning!

Prayer thought: "Ask, and it will be given you; search, and you will find." (Matt. 7:7a)

LESSON 76

Mark 12:12, Fear of the Crowd, and
Mark 12:13-17, Second Clash

In time the hecklers would be back in an attempt to discredit Jesus before the crowd. The thousands of pilgrims in Jerusalem for the Passover complicated the Sanhedrin's plans. The crowds had not forgotten Palm Sunday and all of Jesus' miracles!

The Jews hated the Roman government that ruled over them. The conservative Jews thought it was wrong to pay taxes to a heathen state because some of their money would support heathen temples. The Herodians were a class of Jews that favored the Roman government and opposed the Jews who were hostile to Rome. They were a political group and were the traitors, the Quislings, of Jesus' day. Bitter opposition reigned between the Pharisees and Herodians.[30] Here the enemies of Jesus sent both parties to Jesus to put him to the test. They could not imagine how he could help but offend at least one group. If Jesus agreed with Pharisees, the Herodians would tell Rome. If Jesus agreed with the Herodians, he would offend the Jews because they hated Rome.

Yet, Jesus' answer amazed everyone! Jesus asked for a denarius, the coin stamped with the emperor's head. The poll tax—seventeen cents, the amount of a Roman's daily wage—was paid with this coin. People had to pay taxes for the protection and assistance they received from the government with Caesar's coins. But Jesus also revealed a higher law—allegiance to God. If we bear the image of God, we must live for him. What an answer!

Second Clash:

Who	Question	Jesus' Answer	Effect
Pharisees and Herodians	Loyalty to God or Caesar?	Asked a question, then made a statement	Amazed

Prayer thought: Satan mobilizes everything that he can commandeer in order to hinder our prayer. (*Prayer*, p. 87)

LESSON 77

Mark 12:18-23, Third Clash, and
Mark 12:24-27, God of the Living

The Sadducees were a religious sect that did not believe in resurrection, angels, or spirits, and took the Pentateuch (Genesis-Deuteronomy) as their teaching. They claimed that Moses did not speak about life after death. Jesus, however, cleverly quoted from Exod. 3:6, speaking of Abraham, Isaac, and Jacob in the present tense. The Sadducees' story of the seven husbands showed how foolishly they tried to prove there is no resurrection.

What a terrific answer! Jesus flatly declared that the Sadducees didn't know the Scripture, or the power of God. The Sadducees had referred to the writing of Moses. Jesus did not contradict the law but picked it up with "I am the God of Abraham, Isaac, and Jacob." He made it clear that death is not permanent. Jesus changed death completely! God is living and so are his people. We cannot fully understand it, but we must seek to know the Scriptures and to know the power of God.

I remember once making a remark that I'd never touched a dead body when it was cold. Later when my brother passed away we went to the mortuary. As we stood by the casket, Merrill put his hand on my brother's hand and asked me to do likewise. Carefully I put my hand on my brother's and had the shock of my life. I knew the hand would not be warm, but it was hard as a stone, like a rock! The physical body was dead. Was this what Lazarus was like when Jesus raised him? What power! What glory! Is that what Jesus meant when he said, "He is God not of the dead, but of the living"?

Third Clash:

Who	Question	Jesus' Answer	Effect
Sadducees	Resurrection?	Asked a question, then gave a powerful answer	Silenced

Prayer thought: Prayer is the most important work in the Kingdom of God. (*Prayer*, p. 68)

LESSON 78

Mark 12:28-34, Fourth Clash

It's refreshing to meet this young lawyer. He seemed to have a positive attitude. His question was familiar and often discussed. With 613 commandments, how could anyone know which was the most important?

What a brilliant answer Jesus gave! God doesn't make his laws a burden, for his divine law is summed up in one word—love—love with heart, soul, and mind. Thus, the first table (section) of the Ten Commandments is love to God, the second is love to one's neighbor.

All our problems can be resolved in one word—love. Love is the fulfillment of the whole. If it is obeyed, all other commandments will be fulfilled too.

> The biblical conception of the heart makes it the very center of our being and personality; here also dwells the life or soul; here functions the mind or power to think and from them all results the . . . strength. Since this is God's own commandment, uttered by his own mouth, we have here man's psychology as conceived by man's own Creator, who certainly knows man better than man can know himself.[31]

The first three commandments (as Lutherans and Roman Catholics number them) encompass Deut. 6:5. The rest of the commandments are encompassed by Lev. 19:6.

Fourth Clash:

Who	Question	Jesus' Answer	Effect
One of the scribes	Greatest commandment?	First is to love God, second is to love neighbor	Scribe agreed, people silenced

Prayer thought: Bear . . . in mind . . . the aversion to prayer which we feel more or less strongly from time to time . . . should not make us anxious or bewildered. (*Prayer*, p. 88)

LESSON 79

Mark 12:35-37, Son of David, and
Mark 12:38-40, Long Robes and Prayers

This scene took place on Tuesday afternoon. Matthew 22:41 says that the Pharisees were gathered before Jesus. So was the crowd of eager pilgrims.

Jesus had brilliantly answered four questions. Now he asked a question concerning the Messiah. Is he God? Is he man? Or is he both? The Pharisees taught that the Messiah was to be the Son of David, from David's lineage (Matt. 1:1-17, Luke 3:23-37), but there they stopped. Jesus quoted Psalm 110, which everyone in the crowd knew, with these implied interpretations:

The Lord (Father) said to *my Lord* (Jesus, David's Son)
Sit at *my* (Father's) *right hand*,
until *I* (God) put *your* (Jesus') enemies
under your (Jesus') feet.

Jesus used this Scripture to reveal that Christ, the Messiah, is more than the Son of David, because David recognized him as *Lord.* Christ is both human and divine—the Son of David but also the Son of God. Jesus was making the revelation of himself clearer and clearer. (See Mark 8:29; 10:47-48). His purpose was to win even the Pharisees. He seemed to say, "Do you believe who I am? Shall I prove it by a psalm you love and by David whom you revere?"

Jesus' pure and mighty motive was to put into practice the great commandment of love he had just explained to the lawyer. Jesus concluded these mighty clashes by raising the all-important question, "Who do you say that I am?"

In Mark 12:38-40 Jesus condemned the hypocrisy of the scribes and Pharisees. If you want a fuller picture of their hypocrisy, read Matthew 23. Notice their (1) desire for importance and recognition, (2) greed and dishonesty, and (3) long prayers and emphasis on appearance. Where do we find ourselves here?

Prayer thought: "Likewise the Spirit helps us in our weakness; for we do not know how to pray as we ought, but that very Spirit intercedes with sighs too deep for words." (Rom. 8:26)

LESSON 80

Mark 12:41-44, The Widow's Coins

This was still Tuesday. What a long day of teaching, patience, and love. What a striking contrast the widow was to the religious leaders in the preceding paragraph. Notice Jesus' compassionate yearning to help. He had a deep desire to penetrate into the lives of all questioners.

Jesus must have sat down where he could watch the treasury for a special reason. In the eyes of the world, the widow's gift was very small, worthless. In the eyes of Christ, the widow's gift was tremendous; she gave out of her poverty; it was her whole living. The gift of the Pharisees was almost worthless; they gave out of their abundance. The widow's coins were worth less than half a cent, but it was all she had. The Lord sees our hearts and the love with which we give our gifts. Really, it is not so much the amount we give that Jesus sees as it is the amount we keep for ourselves and the tremendous blessings we miss.

We have now finished Unit 11, Clashes in the Temple, Mark 11:1—12:44. See the outline on pages 10 and 11. Notice Mark's brilliant mind. The first clash was a spiritual question, the second clash a political question, the third clash a physical question, and the fourth clash a moral question.

Prayer thought: Let us pray for our leaders at all times instead of constantly criticizing them. (*Prayer*, p. 73)

LESSON 81

Mark 13:1-2, Not One Stone, and
Mark 13:3-8, Signs in the World

Jesus had left the temple for the last time, two days before the Passover. Sitting on the Mount of Olives, Jesus and his disciples could look across the Kidron Valley to the hill on which the magnificent temple stood, its golden roof sparkling in the rays of the setting sun.

Try to find a description of this magnificent structure in a Bible dictionary or reference book.

Herod had built this temple to appease the Jews when he was appointed governor of Judea. The work started around 20 B.C., which was about sixteen years before the birth of Christ. The construction of the main buildings took about eight years. The courts were not completed until around A.D. 62-64, just a few years before the structure was destroyed. It is said that when the Temple was fired upon the heavy gold plates covering part of it melted and the molten gold ran down into the crevices between the huge marble blocks. The Roman soldiers, in order to get the gold, tore down every one of those massive stones until not one was left resting upon the other.[32]

Jesus needed to talk to the disciples about the future, so once again he took a question and turned it into a revelation of future hope. Their conversation seemed to combine the two big questions of the chapter, judgment of the Jewish nation and judgment of the world.

Prayer thought: We wonder why we see so little fruit as a result of our [prayerless] meetings and our [prayerless] work! Hell laughs and heaven weeps over such meetings. (*Prayer*, p. 74)

LESSON 82

Mark 13:9-13, Signs in the Local Community

Christ's kingdom is not for cowards. One has to take up the cross. How often Jesus' prophecies have been allowed to take place through the years. Acts records many persecutions and how the Lord stood by to help. Throughout church history, many thousands of martyrs have died.

Clearly, these signs were to be fulfilled at that time, but they are also reminders to each age that Christ is coming and that we ought to watch and pray. Think of those today who are suffering for their faith under totalitarian governments. How many will be martyred for their faith in the coming years?

Evangelistic work will reach worldwide, all nations. Our dependence must not be on ourselves—our power, our ability, our money, our wisdom—but on the Holy Spirit of Jesus (John 14:26). The name of Jesus will do it. That name unites or divides.

Prayer thought: "Eternal Father, you gave your Son the name of Jesus to be a sign of our salvation. Plant in every heart the love of the Savior of the world, Jesus Christ our Lord, who lives and reigns with you and the Holy Spirit, one God, now and forever. Amen."[33]

LESSON 83

Mark 13:14-23, Signs in the Church

This was a vivid prophecy of the coming overthrow of the Jewish nation, including the actual overthrow of Jerusalem, the Holy City, by the armies of Rome. These events would scatter the disciples throughout the world and thus spread the gospel to Rome and Asia. "Those in Judea," the Christians, would be forced to leave the country.

They are not to flee to the mountains of Judea, but beyond the Jordan to Perea. The Christians followed this bidding of Jesus. Eusebius 3, 5 reports that the congregation in Jerusalem, following a revelation received by reliable men before the war, migrated to Pella in Perga. As far as one can judge, this must have been at the very time when bloody factions in the city were making an abomination of the temple. When should they flee? When they see the desolating sacrilege of the temple being desecrated by heathen. Something absolutely abominable in God's sight, profaning something sacred. An idol altar was placed on the temple altar for burnt offerings. The blood of 8,500 victims flooded the temple. Read Josephus, *Wars* 4, 5:1-2.[34]

Notice the haste with which the elect must flee. In Palestine much time was spent on the housetop. If that was where one heard the news, one must take the outside stairway and run, not go into the house to gather possessions. Even one moment could prove to be fatal.

The elect are the elect, because God succeeded in bringing them to faith and to heaven ... God wanted to include all men; many absolutely refused.[35]

Notice Jesus' final warning (verses 21-23). Do we in our age ascribe too much power and strength to Satan instead of living in the authority of the name of Jesus? Remember, Satan doesn't care what is said as long as he's in the foreground! Jesus warns that Satan's tactics will be so convincing that it will be difficult not to fall away unless we are in the Word and focused on Jesus!

Prayer thought: The Spirit calls us to do the quiet, difficult, trying work of boring holy explosive material into the souls of the unconverted by daily and unceasing prayer. (*Prayer*, p. 77)

LESSON 84

Mark 13:24-27, Signs in the Sky, and
Mark 13:28-31, The Fig Tree

"In those days" means the end of the world (Isa. 13:10, Joel 2:30-31; 3:14-15). The last days will arrive and end all tribulation. Mysteriously, the very forces of nature will be shaken. Then the Son will appear: the event for which all Christendom has been waiting. His great promise is that when these things happen, he will come for his elect, using his mighty servants, the angels.

Are we to fear and tremble as we await his coming? No, we are to live in awe of God's holiness and righteousness compared to our own unworthiness. While prophecy unrolls a picture of dread, it is bright with the glorious hope in Christ for all who trust in him. Praise him for it! Think how the persecuted, suffering, lonely disciples of Jesus are even now praying, "Come, Lord Jesus!" Are we?

In verses 28-31, Jesus tried to show that the events that would soon take place were part of a larger plan that had a sequence, an order. Jesus always used something with which the people were familiar. Fig trees grew everywhere in Palestine.

Prayer thought: If the Spirit of prayer can give us real zeal for souls, we will want to have a part in praying for an awakening. (*Prayer*, p. 77)

LESSON 85

Mark 13:32-37, Keep Alert

Imagine! Jesus' human nature did not know when he would come again! Of course, in his oneness of the Father, Son, and Holy Spirit, Jesus knew all things, but he did not use his divine attributes except as he needed them in his work in union with the Father here on earth.

Watch! Beware! Keep alert! Jesus issued these warnings repeatedly. Are we living in the Word daily? Are we praying and interceding for others? Are we going to other nations with the gospel? Are we talking about his coming and living it?

An old man had one room, but every evening as he retired, his clothes were put away perfectly, his shoes stood in perfect order. When asked why, he answered, "This is one way I am on watch, and always pray, 'Come, Lord Jesus.'"

We have now finished Unit 12, Future Events, Mark 13:1-37. See the outline on pages 10 and 11.

Prayer thought: We should enter into this work [of prayer] and become personal and regular interceders for certain definite individuals. (*Prayer*, p. 79)

LESSON 86

Mark 14:1-2, Plot to Kill, and
Mark 14:3-9, The Anointing

As we study this word of Christ's passion, let us remember we are standing on holy ground. The divine foreknowledge of our Lord is striking against the darkness of his enemies. Think of the spiritual condition of the leaders and keep in mind the sharp contrast of Jesus' love and their hate.

The day was Tuesday and Passover was on Thursday. The Passover commemorated God's preservation of the Hebrews in Egypt, when he took them out of bondage and slavery after 430 years. It was celebrated every year. In each family, the father chose a lamb, a year-old male, without blemish or spot. The lamb was killed before the altar and the blood was sprinkled on the doorposts of the family's home. Then the lamb was roasted whole in the oven, supported by two sticks that formed a cross. For the Passover meal, the lamb was served with wine, bitter herbs, and unleavened bread. Any food left over was to be burned. (See Exod. 12:1-36.)

The ignorance of the schemers about Jesus' timing was so pronounced. Nearly half a million people were in Jerusalem because of the Passover feast. Jesus knew the precise day and hour he wanted to be crucified—sacrificed as the Passover Lamb. Thus, he would upset the plans of his enemies!

Notice the sharp contrast of Mark 14:1-2 (hate) with 14:3-9 (love). John (12:1-8) tells us that the anointing happened six days before the Passover. Why Mark took it out of chronological order, we do not know. Possibly he wanted to show this beautiful story of love in direct contrast to the ugly, hateful deeds of the chief priests, scribes, and Judas.

Mark's Gospel says this deed was performed in Simon the leper's home. Perhaps Simon's home was larger than those of Jesus' other friends. Notice the beauty of this woman's deed, "She has done what she could; she has anointed my body beforehand for its burial."

The woman used an alabaster jar filled with nard. Alabaster was white and often translucent. Nard was an aromatic plant from which ointment was made. It was very expensive. This ointment could have been sold for three hundred denari, almost a year's salary! The woman's love, however, was so devoted that she never defended herself. Jesus' defense of her was beautiful. He simply said, "Let her alone." If we truly give in love, no gift to Jesus is too big or too little. Once again, Jesus rewarded the faithful, not the famous.

Prayer thought: We are inclined to think that when we are real busy in the work of the Kingdom of God, then we can without danger spend less time in prayer. (*Prayer*, p. 80)

LESSON 87

Mark 14:10-11, Judas' Plot, and
Mark 14:12-16, The Passover

The plot to kill Jesus thickens! Don't you think it wasn't traumatic! Matthew 26:15 mentions the sum for which Judas betrayed Jesus, thirty pieces of silver, which was the price of a slave (Exod. 21:32).

Judas had talked, eaten, walked, and worshiped with Jesus. He had seen many miracles but had never given up his love for money. Remember, Judas is just an example of what any of us could do if we try to live as Christians but refuse to relinquish our sins to Jesus.

Mark's Gospel takes us from Tuesday evening to Thursday. Not a word is said about Wednesday. Did Jesus spend it teaching his disciples or fasting and talking to the Father?

Jesus had many dear friends in Jerusalem. One answer to the question as to why Jesus kept the man's name and location of his house secret is that his enemies were not to know, not to be able to find out where Jesus would celebrate this Passover in perfect security, right in the city of Jerusalem itself and at night. Try to comprehend what the Lord's Supper meant to the disciples that blessed evening and what it has meant to the Christian church throughout the ages!

The man carrying water was likely the servant of the owner of the house who was probably a friend of Jesus! Usually women carried the water and they generally did so in the morning or evening. Both the time and person seem out of line, so the two disciples, Peter and John (Luke 22:8), could easily have followed Jesus' directions. Peter and John must have been busy—setting the table, getting the bread, herbs, and lamb, and preparing the food ceremonially.

Prayer thought: Prayer ... can remove mountains in our own life and in the lives of others. (*Prayer*, p. 80)

LESSON 88

Mark 14:17-21, Is It I? and
Mark 14:22-25, The Lord's Supper

Jesus had kept the location of the upper room from all the disciples except Peter and John until the appointed time. He wanted no interruptions—no arrests or disturbances. He had the greatest messages to deliver to his disciples: one that would not be understood now, but would be a great comfort in days to come.

Mark's account begins on Thursday evening, about 6:00, with the meal in progress. Do you think Jesus was giving Judas another chance? Just think, Judas was one of them. Wasn't he shocked by his guilt? He sold the truth for money!

A deep examination of mind and heart was necessary for the disciples when Jesus made his shocking announcement. "Lord, who is it?" they asked (John 13:25). Each might have wondered, "Am I the one?" Likewise, we need to examine ourselves. Is the Lord's Supper becoming too commonplace that we forget the presence of Christ, the preparation of our heart and mind?

Mark's action verbs are picturesque—eating, took, blessing, broke, gave, said, take, giving thanks, drank, poured. Notice that Jesus used again and again the present-tense verb *is*. Jesus introduced something so new, so glorious, that only eternity can grasp it.

The old covenant had been sealed with the sacrifice and blood of animals (Exod. 24:4-8). The old covenant had been written in animal blood and pointed forward to fulfillment. The new covenant was written in the blood of the Son of God who was the complete fulfillment of the promise, the purchase of our redemption. Christ, our Servant, the once-and-for-all Lamb, did away with the Passover lamb.

Christ instituted a new supper, the Lord's Supper, by which we may partake of the body and blood of the Lamb. Jesus said, "This is my body; this is my blood" (1 Cor. 11:23-25). With those words, he forgives us all our sins and tells us to remember him and his mighty sacrifice. Yes, the body and blood of Christ is in, with, and under the earthly elements, the bread and wine, that carry this spiritual blessing into body and soul. Although we don't know how this is so, Jesus said it was true, so in faith we can experience his truth. The Lord's Supper gives us as much strength as we will take!

A woman who hadn't heard of Christ was converted and received Christ with joy. Her first Communion was an inspiration to the whole congregation. Her face was crowned with joy and tears, "His body and blood for me!" She was trying to grasp the holy moment.

Prayer thought: By prayer ... we couple the powers of heaven to our helplessness ... the powers which can sleep in sin and raise up the head. (*Prayer*, p. 81)

LESSON 89

Mark 14:26-31, Prediction, and
Mark 14:32-42, Gethsemane

Leave it to Mark to open the first paragraph here on such an upbeat thought—a hymn. Review all that had transpired this day and Jesus' foreknowledge of what will take place. Jesus was in perfect control. As Jesus led his eleven to the Garden of Gethsemane he not only heroically told them of their failure, but also gave his sheep two tremendous promises. Yes, the shepherd will be struck down as predicted, but the shepherd will rise, and they—the sheep—shall see him!

Peter, however, in proud confidence, seemed to have been thinking of only one thing. With courage and devotion he claimed he would not forsake Jesus, even if the other ten did. Do you think Peter had been so touched by the solemn service of the Lord's Supper and loved Jesus so much that he was even ready to die?

Gethsemane—what a holy place! In 1951, when Merrill spent three months walking the paths Jesus had walked, Gethsemane was his favorite spot. He would go to the Garden of Gethsemane at midnight, at three in the morning, and often at sunrise. Reading the Gospels by the light of the moon in that garden became very meaningful and precious.

There at Gethsemane Jesus shrank from sin. He did not draw away from the physical cross; martyrs and thieves died on the cross too. Sin was the source of his horror. If Christ had not shrunk from sin, he could not have been the Son of God, for holiness cannot endure sin. Even God turned away from Jesus because of sin. Can you begin to comprehend what Christ's alienation from God meant (Isa. 53:10)?

How God must love us not to have answered Christ's prayer in removing the cup. How it must have broken the Father's heart. Although the cup was not removed, God's grace was poured out so that death lost its power, the grave lost its sting, and Jesus went on to victory! After his prayer, Christ was ready. He was physically worn out, having crucified self, but God's grace sustained him. He was ready to face the cross!

Do you know that Christianity is the only religion of a suffering God? It presents a God who suffers, who suffers with every sick person ... the one who sees all the horrors of the world most clearly is God himself, and that he suffers from all evil, and all suffering of humanity."[36]

Prayer thought: By prayer ... we couple the powers of heaven to our helplessness ... the powers which can capture strongholds and make the impossible possible. (*Prayer*, p. 81)

LESSON 90

Mark 14:43-50, Betrayal; Mark 14:51-52, Young Man; and Mark 14:53-65, Trial before the High Priest

Judas's work was almost over—what depth of darkness! He completed his cowardly, base crime in Gethsemane, a place where he knew his Master would go for prayer.

Rome ruled Israel, but the Jews were given some authority over religious matters. "About two hundred soldiers, and certainly as many temple police, together with a nondescript rabbi that came along to see the excitement, block the entrance to Gethsemane."[37]

For some reason Mark omitted mentioning that the whole army fell to the ground at Jesus' words (John 18:6), but Jesus mastered the situation perfectly and all that occurred did so only with his consent. Remember, God was putting into action what he had prophesied through the prophets. Jesus voluntarily put himself into the enemies' hands.

Some think the young man was Mark, for he was the only Gospel writer to have recorded this incident. We do not know for certain who the man was.

It was midnight when the mob arrested Jesus in the garden. How many trials did Jesus have? We will look at five! Mark did not record the first one before Annas (John 18:19-24), but he recorded the second trial before Caiaphas.

Do you notice that many bore false witness against Jesus, but they did not agree? Jesus was innocent. Every accusation was a lie! Hence,

Caiaphas became desperate. He had to have Jesus condemned. Jesus' silence infuriated Caiaphas. The judges as well as Jesus realized that no evidence had been given to warrant a reply. The witnesses showed that Jesus was absolutely innocent. The silence screamed out that this trial was illegal. The innocence of Jesus could make no reply.

Then Caiaphas boldly presented the real issue. Was Jesus the Messiah? Jesus gave a clear-cut answer that impressed his judges with the reality of the One they had before them. The powerful "I am" resounded through the judgment hall, and Jesus emphasized it with a quotation from Daniel (Dan. 7:13). Even the judges recognized this as a prophecy about the Messiah. However, his answer made Caiaphas even more furious. The verdict should have been the court's, but Caiaphas took the decision into his own hands. He shouted and tore his clothes to show his horror at the "blasphemy."

Prayer thought: Observe the situation in the Christian enterprises of today. That the machinery has become too heavy is due to the fact that we are operating it with human labor instead of running it by power from above. (*Prayer*, pp. 85–86)

LESSON 91

Mark 14:66-72, The Denial, and
Mark 15:1-5, Trial before Pilate

In the courtyards of the high priest's palace, a clever servant-girl got the best of the chief of the twelve disciples. Surely Peter truly loved his Lord and expressed his devotion to Jesus often, but he was always too self-confident. Now he was scared, stunned, tired, in danger, and lonely. The turn of events had come too fast. Even his dress and speech betrayed him as a Galilean, a follower of Jesus. Losing his temper, Peter stooped to the lowest—cursing, swearing, and insisting, "I do not know the man!" (Matt. 26:74). But Jesus had prepared Peter for this (Matt. 26:75). Peter was utterly convicted, and repentance and tears later brought forgiveness and peace.

Mark 15:1-5 tells about Jesus' third trial. Caiaphas had to wait until morning for this trial, even if he had declared Jesus to be deserving of death, because the Jews were not allowed to pronounce capital punishment (John 18:31). Pilate was a Roman. Rome had conquered Palestine and ruled over it with an iron hand. The Jews were afraid of Pilate because Pilate was provoked at their constant bickering. For this trial they trumped up charges against Jesus of not paying taxes, wanting to be king, and even heading up riots. Pilate tried to evade the verdict of Jesus' death by sending Jesus to Herod's court (Luke 23:6, the fourth trial), because Jesus' home was in Galilee, which was under Herod's jurisdiction.

The seventy-one men who made up the Sanhedrin had been called out of bed at an unearthly hour for the first trial before Annas and the second trial before Caiaphas. All judges did not have to be present at every session so Nicodemus and Joseph of Arimathea (see John 19:38-42) may not have been there. Imagine the council's impatience as they had to wait to have the third trial before Pilate, the governor. The Sanhedrin could decree death, but only the Roman government could execute it (Mark 10:33). These religious leaders were anxious that Pilate grant their unreasonable request before their Sabbath began at 6:00 in the evening.

A lawyer who has studied Jesus' trial has found forty-five illegal points: No two witnesses agreed, it was conducted at night and during a Jewish feast, Caiaphas questioned the prisoner, the death penalty had to be passed at a second session on another day, there were false witnesses, and no witnesses on Jesus' side, Jesus was a Galilean, and many others. But the Servant was in full command. Everything progressed as prophesied.

Prayer thought: The labor of prayer requires a definite plan and purpose. (*Prayer*, p. 82)

LESSON 92

Mark 15:6-15, Barabbas

Note the emotional intensity of this crowd—the murderer Barabbas, the vicious Jewish council, the unbelievably fickle mob that before had so enthusiastically praised Jesus, the spineless Pilate, the supreme calm majesty and power of Jesus. Imagine how the proud Sanhedrin must have boiled in anger at the name *king of the Jews*.

Pilate had the awful task of pronouncing the execution: death on the cross. To the Roman mind, crucifixion was the most despised and humiliating death. However, the Jewish leaders wanted this humiliation (Deut. 21:23: "anyone hung on a tree is under God's curse").

> The mob spirit was beginning to rise, a terrible thing especially in the East. The more they yelled, the more agitated the scene became. Even now one word from Pilate could have gained control—a sharp military order to the chiliarch of the cohort of 600 legionaries to clear the place of Jews in short order, and to protect Jesus from molestation. But Pilate was long past such a courageous course of action.[38]
>
> Scourging or flogging is when a person is stripped of clothes, the body bent forward across a low pillar, the back stretched and exposed to the blows. To hold the body in position the victim's hands must have been tied to rings in the floor ... and the feet to rings behind. The Romans used short handled whips, each with several leather lashes, ugly acorn shaped pieces of lead ... or bone fastened to the end of each short lash.[39]

What a gruesome picture!

We have completed Unit 13, The Arrest and Trial, Mark 14:1— 15:15, a unit of contrasts. See pages 10 and 11.

Prayer thought: Lack of proper planning will be enough to make the prayer life of many unproductive and ineffective. (*Prayer*, p. 82)

LESSON 93

Mark 15:16-20, The Mockery

The mockery of Jesus makes the mind stagger with shame. How could a mockery like this be carried on? It wasn't normal. The flogging took place outside the Praetorium before the Jewish mob and Pilate. Next, the soldiers, on Pilate's order, took Jesus inside, where they made him as unlike a king as possible.

On Jesus' aching back the soldiers placed a scarlet robe. Probably there was a thornbush in the courtyard and they laughingly twisted a crown of thorns from the stems of the bush and pressed it into his head. With sarcasm, they put a reed (a scepter) into his hand. Striking his face with their hands and hitting the scepter against his crown and head must have caused excruciating pain (Matt. 27:27-31). The purple robe and crown symbolized a king's power. Here the bitter hate and scorn the Romans hate for a Jew is revealed.

How could Jesus have restrained himself? He, the true King, with all power, could have ended the mockery. Oh, what the Servant endured for you and me (Phil. 2:8).

Martin Luther mentions five steps in Jesus' humiliation: his birth in poverty, his suffering, the crucifixion, his death, his burial.[40]

Prayer Thought: "Father, forgive them; for they do not know what they are doing." (Luke 23:34)

LESSON 94

Mark 15:21-24, Golgotha, and
Mark 15:25-32, The Crucifixion

Mark 10:45, the key verse, gives us the outstanding statement, "For the Son of Man came not to be served, but to serve, and to give his life as a ransom for many." These final lessons show us the magnitude of Jesus' suffering and death, all done out of love so that we might have life.

No Roman soldier would lower himself to carry a cross for a criminal, and no Jew would willingly touch a cross. So Simon was enlisted for the job. We don't know much about him. Mark 15:21 tells us Simon was from Cyrene (in North Africa) and the father of Alexander and Rufus, who were known in the early church (Rom. 16:13). It is believed that Christ's close contact with Simon as he carried the cross up the hill led to Simon's conversion. His sons later became zealous workers in the kingdom. But even on the way to the gruesome cross, Jesus touched another nation!

As you study Paragraph 3, notice that Jesus was still in control. Pilate took his revenge on the Jews by proclaiming Jesus as King—in three languages (John 19:20). Crucifixion was a gruesome, shameful form of capital punishment—the "reward" for rebellion and crime. Only slaves or non-Romans were crucified. Jesus was first called the king of the Jews in Matt. 2:2 and this was the crime emblazoned on his cross.

Interestingly, the people ironically pronounced the truth as Jesus hung on the cross. The temple of his body was raised in three days (verse 29). The scribes and priests said, "Let the Messiah come down." Jesus was the Christ, but spiritual blindness blocked their vision. Caiaphas was so concerned about the earthly temple he could not see the temple of Jesus' body.

It was often customary to give persons to be crucified drugged wine to deaden their feelings. Jesus, however, refused to accept it. He wanted his mind to be clear. The messages that were to be spoken on the cross must not be lost. Jesus did all this because he loves us!

Prayer thought:

> O sacred head, now wounded,
> With grief and shame weighed down,
> Now scornfully surrounded
> With thorns, thine only crown;
> O sacred head, what glory,
> What bliss till now was thine!
> Yet, though despised and gory,
> I joy to call thee mine.

Attributed to Bernard of Clairvaux, 1091-1153; Paul Gerhardt, 1607-1676; trans. composite, alt.

LESSON 95

Mark 15:33-39, Death, and
Mark 15:40-41, The Women

The Jews measured time beginning at six o'clock in the morning, so the third hour (mentioned in many versions of the Bible) was nine o'clock, the sixth hour was twelve o'clock, and the ninth hour was three o'clock.

The darkness signified God's judgment. Jesus suffered all alone and in silence with the cloud of all of humanity's sins on him. This load of sin separated him from the Father. God can't tolerate sin and now it was heaped on his Son. Jesus, who had lived so close to the Father, experienced being forsaken. It was this experience that made him cry out, "My God, my God, why have you forsaken me?"

In the garden, God heard and strengthened Jesus. Here on the cross, God turned away from him for he was made sin for us. Imagine those three dark hours! Psalm 22 foretells the agony of Jesus' death. His physical death was gruesome, but his spiritual separation from the Father when he took our sins on himself was the ultimate sacrifice. He who was so close to the Father had to be separated! What a ransom! Thanks be to God who laid on him the iniquity of us all! (Isa. 53:6).

Jesus was silent, but then God spoke. The curtain in the temple was torn in two. The Holy of Holies (Lev. 16:34) became open to all people. It was no longer the place where only the high priest dared to enter once a year. Jesus had paid the sacrifice for sin. He had become the Lamb. Through his name, all people have direct access to God. The rending of the temple curtain must have been a frightening experience for the priests who were preparing the evening sacrifices.

At a distance from the cross, a cluster of women watched the gruesome events. These women perhaps lingered long enough to see where Jesus' precious body was laid. How they must have recalled Jesus' love and compassion shown to each of them. Here we see their devotion and their overwhelming love.

Prayer thought:

Calvary's mournful mountain climb,
There, adoring at his feet,
Mark that miracle of time,
God's own sacrifice complete.
"It is finished!" hear him cry;
Learn from Jesus Christ to die.

James Montgomery, 1771-1854

LESSON 96

Mark 15:42-47, Burial

Jesus' friends and relatives were unprepared to bury Jesus. Would the soldiers simply drag his body away? No, God had provided for the care of his Son's body through Joseph.

Preparation Day (Friday) was the day before the Sabbath. Jesus' body had to be quickly taken down from the cross, the nails pulled out, the bruised body wrapped and buried before the Sabbath began at 6:00. God had two faithful servants from the council who performed the task at great personal risk. The Jews had threatened to expel anyone from the synagogue who confessed Jesus or had any connection with him. Also, touching a dead body made a person ceremonially unclean. Imagine the courage of Joseph and Nicodemus, and how they must have suffered throughout Jesus' last days.

The lesson asks how Mark described Joseph. He was from Arimathea and a respected member of the council. Joseph was looking for the kingdom of God. A man of courage, Joseph faced Pilate to ask for Jesus' body. Matthew 27:57 also reveals that he was a rich man, and Luke 23:50 says he was a good and righteous man who did not consent to Jesus' death. The Son of God, who was Servant and Master to the end, was buried by a ruler with dignity (Isa. 53:9). However, there was no fanfare or display, so it was important that the women saw where Joseph laid him.

Prayer thought: It is difficult for the Lord to get enough people to carry on the work of prayer. (*Prayer*, p. 86)

LESSON 97

Mark 16:1-8, The Resurrection

A new era has begun! If you or I had told this story, it would have been full of superlatives but not so with Mark. Jesus' death and resurrection was fact, and Mark expressed it plainly. The Jewish Sabbath was Saturday, so the women had to wait until the first day of the week to honor the body of Jesus by anointing it and finishing the burial. In Palestine, it was necessary to bury the bodies immediately because of the climate and the difficulty of preserving the remains. Every hour counted. The women wanted to prepare the body while it was still in good enough condition to be handled.

It was very early and John 20:1 tells us it was still dark. The women were concerned about the big, flat, round stone that rolled into a groove and covered the entrance to the tomb. As soon as Mary saw the stone rolled away, she did not even stop to examine the tomb, but rushed away to tell the disciples (John 20:2). The other women were filled with fear as they received a startling message.

Imagine what the women saw when the angel spoke, saying, "He is not here; can't you see? Look, look at the place where he would be lying. There are the clothes, the napkin. A body, a spirit has risen!" What did the women think, fear, and hope? Were they aware that they were looking at a miracle—the miracle of miracles? The women told no one except those the angel designated—the disciples and Peter. Notice how lovingly Peter was reinstated. He needed the extra assurance.

> Silently, invisibly, wondrously, gloriously the living body passed through the rock. When the tomb was empty, the angel came and opened the tomb to show that it was indeed empty....A new era has begun, heaven and earth are now joined, for Christ, our Savior, has risen! The wall of separation (sin) has fallen; God is reconciled to men; the sacrifice of the Son has been accepted by the Father. This is the supreme Easter truth.[41]

Death is swallowed up in victory (1 Cor. 15:54).

Prayer thought:
> Early hasten to the tomb
> Where they laid his breathless clay;
> All is solitude and gloom.
> Who has taken him away?
> Christ is ris'n! He meets our eyes.
> Savior, teach us so to rise.

LESSON 98

Mark 16:9-11, First Appearance;
Mark 16:12-13, Second Appearance; and
Mark 16:14-18, Go, Tell

The closing verses of Mark are sometimes believed to have been added later. We don't know if they were written by Mark or not, but they are true and fit in with the other Gospel writers. They also form a wonderful conclusion to Mark's tremendous Gospel. In his conclusion, Mark recorded three of Christ's appearances and showed how the disciples slowly accepted that Jesus did rise again (8:31; 9:31; 10:34).

First Appearance:
According to John 20, Mary Magdalene, the leader of the women, did not stop at the tomb as the other women did, but ran to tell Peter and the other disciples. The disciples were probably hiding in a room somewhere. They were frightened, but were also trying to remember what Jesus had told them. After hearing Mary's startling news, two disciples, Peter and John, ran to the tomb. John 20 implies it would take a while for them to understand Jesus had risen from the dead. Mary returned to the tomb and stood there weeping. She was the first to meet Jesus, but in her blind sorrow at first thought Jesus was the gardener. Only when he spoke her name did the wonderful truth dawn on her that Jesus was alive!

Second Appearance:
We don't think that Jesus always appeared in the same glorified form during the forty-day period he was on earth following his resurrection.

Notice the words *"they did not believe them"* (verse 13) when the two who had seen Jesus returned to the other disciples.

Go Tell:

There are ten or eleven recorded appearances of Jesus, but Mark recorded Jesus' appearance to one disciple, then two, and then the eleven. The disciples had refused to grasp the evidence the women brought them. Jesus rebuked them for this. Having themselves beheld the Lord, the disciples were ready to be true witnesses. So Jesus gave them the Great Commission (Mark 16:15). No longer was any person, Jew or Gentile, to be shut out from the gospel—only those who chose to refuse its good news. "Christianity is the one religion which does not demand that the sinner save himself, but that he permit the Son of God to save him and go out in power."[42]

Again, as Jesus sent the disciples out, we are reminded of those power-packed words *My name* (verse 17). What does Jesus' name mean to you? Are we as individuals, a church, and a nation powerless because we don't know or experience the power of Jesus' name? His name is so important today with the prevalence of the cults and satanic worship. His name has all authority (Matt. 28:18).

This faith is not for shallow, easy believers. God's grace is so wide and so deep that only eternity will reveal its immensity. *Believe* in the Greek means action, and the Great Commission calls us to be active.

Prayer thought: Take plenty of time before you begin to speak with God. . . . Give God time to play the prelude to prayer for the benefit of your distracted soul. (*Prayer*, p. 94)

LESSON 99

Mark 16:19-20, The Ascension

Mark stated only a few facts about Jesus' forty days on earth between the resurrection and ascension. The disciples often saw Jesus appear and disappear during this time, but he had never before left in this way—"taken up into heaven." Our Lord could have ascended into heaven without any human eye seeing him. Can you imagine the joy for the disciples who witnessed his ascension?

Jesus has now completed his work of redemption and is seated at the right hand of the Father. He has all authority and has fulfilled the work of Prophet, High Priest, and King. He is now our King.

Jesus' place at the right hand of God (a symbol of power) was prophesied (Psalm 110). Its fulfillment was also recorded extensively (Rom. 8:34, Eph. 1:20, Col. 3:1, Heb. 1:3, 1 Pet. 3:22, Rev. 3:21). We may wonder what Jesus' work is now. Martin Luther says that he protects his kingdom from its enemies, prays for us, and sends us his Holy Spirit.[43]

Heaven! How we need to be excited, longing to be with Jesus! One evening as I put my grandchildren to bed Joshua, eight years old, said, "Oh, Grandma, I have a story to tell you! In Sunday school we saw a big picture of Jesus going into heaven. And, do you know, he's soon coming back like that! When he comes all the graves are going to pop open and all the people, hundreds of people, will come out. They are going to fly in the sky, and then Jesus will reach out his hand and ask us to come with him. And do you know the first thing I'm going to ask Jesus is if I can have a tea party with Grandpa again." What a beautiful witness that Sunday school teacher had been! She must have been excited about Jesus' second coming.

We have completed Unit 14, Crucifixion and Resurrection, Mark 15:16—16:20. See the outline, pages 10 and 11.

Prayer thought:
He is arisen!
Glorious Word!
Now reconciled is God, my Lord;
The gates of heav'n are open.
My Jesus rose triumphantly,
And Satan's arrows broken lie,
Destroyed hell's fiercest weapon.
Oh, hear, what cheer!
Christ victorious,
Rising glorious,
Life is giving.
He was dead, but now is living!

Birgitte K. Boye, 1742-1824; trans. George T. Rygh, 1860-1942, alt.

LESSON 100

Congratulations! You've completed a study of the Gospel of Mark. My continued prayer is that this study will help you see Jesus' life as a powerful, action-filled life that is meaningful for you. Study and share this word together with your family or a small group.

> May the spirit of the Lord rest on you,
> the spirit of wisdom and understanding,
> the spirit of counsel and might,
> the spirit of knowledge and the fear of the Lord.
>
> Isa. 11:2

The Gospel of Mark always brings to mind a story Merrill used to tell. An artist was asked to paint a dead church, a church that had lost Christ's last command, "Go, tell." What did the artist paint? On his canvas was the interior of a large, beautifully and tastefully decorated church. Toward the back of the church hung a box with a sign, "Missions." Over the slot, however, were many cobwebs. "Go, tell!"

ENDNOTES

1. O. Hallesby, *Prayer*, trans. Clarence J. Carlsen (Minneapolis: Augsburg Publishing House, 1975).

2. Merrill Gilbertson, *The Way It Was in Bible Times* (Minneapolis: Augsburg Publishing House, 1959), 66.

3. Sheldon and Sharon Graff, South America, letter, 1990.

4. Gilbertson, *The Way It Was in Bible Times*, 13.

5. Ibid., 14.

6. Charles Erdman, *The Gospel of Mark* (Philadelphia: Westminster Press, 1929), 58.

7. R. C. H. Lenski, *The Interpretation of St. Mark's Gospel* (Columbus: Lutheran Book Concern, 1934), 98.

8. Theodore G. Tappert, editor, *The Book of Concord*, "The Small Catechism" (Philadelphia: Fortress Press, 1959), 345.

9. Lenski, *The Interpretation of St. Mark's Gospel*, 112.

10. Gilbertson, *The Way It Was in Bible Times*, 118.

11. Lenski, *The Interpretation of St. Mark's Gospel*, 122.

12. Erdman, *The Gospel of Mark*, 80.

13. Merrill F. Unger, *Bible Handbook* (Chicago: Moody Press, 1967), 499.

14. Ibid.

15. Ibid.

16. Lenski, *The Interpretation of St. Mark's Gospel*, 133.

17. John Oxenham, Used by permission.

18. Lenski, *The Interpretation of St. Mark's Gospel*, 145.

19. Ibid., 174.

20. Tappert, *The Book of Concord*, 349.

21. J. S. Bergon and S. Marie Schwan, *Surrender: A Guide for Prayer* (Winona, MN: Saint Mary's Press, Christian Brothers' Publications), 17.

22. Mary Basonquet, *The Life and Death of Dietrich Bonhoeffer* (New York: Harper & Row, 1968), 189.

23. Chuck Colson, *Life Sentence* (Old Tappan, N. J.: Fleming H. Revell, 1979), 149.

24. Hallesby, *Prayer*, 30.

25. Colson, *Life Sentence*, 71.

26. Lenski, *The Interpretation of St. Mark's Gospel*, 279.

27. Ibid., 288.

28. Ibid., 290.

29. Ibid., 305.

30. Gilbertson, *The Way It Was in Bible Times*, 89.

31. Lenski, *The Interpretation of St. Mark's Gospel*, 339.

32. Gilbertson, *The Way It Was in Bible Times*, 64.

33. Daily reading for January 1, 1990, *For the Week* (Minneapolis: Augsburg Fortress, 1990).

34. Lenski, *The Interpretation of St. Mark's Gospel*, 362–363.

35. Ibid.

36. Paul Tournier, *A Listening Ear* (Minneapolis: Augsburg Publishing House, 1986), 87.

37. Lenski, *The Interpretation of St. Mark's Gospel*, 407.

38. Ibid., 434.

39. Ibid., 435.

40. Joseph Stump, *Luther's Catechism* (Philadelphia: Fortress Press, 1960), 78–79.

41. Lenski, *The Interpretation of St. Mark's Gospel*, 465.

42. Ibid., 481.

43. Tappert, *The Book of Concord*, 414.

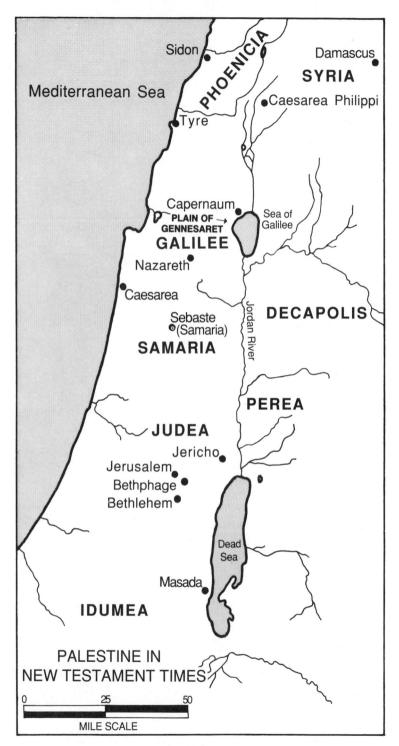

Sidon

Damascus

PHOENICIA

SYRIA

Mediterranean Sea

Caesarea Philippi

Tyre

Capernaum

Sea of Galilee

PLAIN OF GENNESARET →

GALILEE

Nazareth

DECAPOLIS

Caesarea

Sebaste (Samaria)

Jordan River

SAMARIA

PEREA

JUDEA

Jericho

Jerusalem
Bethphage
Bethlehem

Dead Sea

Masada

IDUMEA

PALESTINE IN
NEW TESTAMENT TIMES

0   25   50

MILE SCALE